Berry
720 W. Church
Pl-4-2505

Lord, bless us as we seek
to share;
The blessings of this hour;
Fill us with gratitude
to thee
For thy great love and
power. Amen

ADULT DEVOTIONS

ADULT DEVOTIONS

FOR PUBLIC AND PRIVATE USE

by

Wallace
Fridy

Abingdon Press

NEW YORK • NASHVILLE

ADULT DEVOTIONS

Copyright © 1961 by Abingdon Press

Library of Congress Catalog Card Number: 61-6475

B

SET UP, PRINTED, AND BOUND BY THE
PARTHENON PRESS, AT NASHVILLE,
TENNESSEE, UNITED STATES OF AMERICA

To P. B. Holtzendorff, Jr.,

Affectionately known as "Holtzy,"
Who through his life has shown many of us the "Way"

PREFACE

These devotional messages have all been used in
amplified form as sermons trying to speak to special needs
of a particular group of people. Of course, as with most
sermons, they first spoke to the minister's own need and
then were shared with his people. And it is hoped that
since they have arisen out of the daily experiences of life,
they may have a message for you who read them and
who use them.

They were prepared for personal use, as well as re-
source material for those responsible for leading worship
services. It is hoped, too, that they may be suggestive as
sermon ideas for busy pastors.

At the end of each chapter are worship aids to assist the
leader in conducting a worship service. There are hymn
and scripture suggestions, in addition to a prayer. These
prayers have all been used in public worship. In one of her
books, Margueritte Harmon Bro tells of an old newspaper
clipping in which someone wrote about going to an artist's
studio to see a new painting. He was first guided into a
dark waiting room and left for ten minutes. Then the
artist himself came in and explained saying, "I knew if

you came into the studio with the glare of the street in your eyes, you couldn't possibly get the color values."

This suggests to us that we need to find a time and a place where we can pull apart from the noise and glare of daily living and there find God. It may be in a chapel, a church, an attic, a secluded spot in a park. It may be in solitude or in company with others. It may be in the early morning hours, at noonday, or when the shadows have lengthened and night has come. It can be a time of inspiration when the glare and glitter of the streets are erased from our eyes and we can see life in clearer perspective. It can be a place of renewal.

It is hoped that this book may help many a traveler get the glare out of his eyes and be drawn closer to the Father of us all.

WALLACE FRIDY

CONTENTS

9

Faith that needs no explanation

ALFRED H. FREEMAN HAS WELL SAID THAT "PAUL'S faith is a confidence in God so deep that God does not have to explain His actions in order to hold his love." What higher kind of faith can a person have?

Paul expressed this faith in words found in II Tim. 1:12 when he wrote to his young friend Timothy: "I know whom I have believed, and am persuaded that he is able to keep that which I have committed unto him against that day."

Paul wrote this notwithstanding the fact that his life since becoming a Christian had been fraught with great hardship. Almost from the first moment that he accepted Christ hardships were his. His Christian life started in flight as he escaped the angry mob in Damascus by being lowered in a basket through a hole in the city wall. In spite of all his sufferings and thwarted dreams he forged a faith in God that did not ask for explanation in the face of trial and tribulation.

Writing from a prison cell in Rome, he must have relived all that had happened to him during those eventful years. He knew that his days were numbered, but he gloried in what had happened to him and how his life

11

had been changed. Surely he recalled how he had started out relentless in his determination to persecute the Christians, and how on that lonely Damascan road he had had a vision which resulted in a changed life. Surely he could feel even now the sting that came when a stone had been thrown in hatred at him and had left an ugly scar on his face. Then there were the lashes and the rods which had cut his back. He could never forget the storm-tossed days on an ocean voyage and the shipwreck which had almost cost him his life.

But facing the executioners who would soon knock at his door, he could write from his prison cell: "I know whom I have believed, and am persuaded that he is able to keep that which I have committed unto him against that day."

He did not question why God allowed it to happen any more than he questioned Stephen's stoning, which he had witnessed in Jerusalem before his conversion. He did not demand that God should give him reasons for all that was unwanted which had come his way; he simply trusted. Paul knew that God had his interest at heart and that there was nothing too good to believe about him.

What a lesson this is for us today! Is it not the mark of true friendship when a man has such confidence in a friend that he does not need an explanation for all that happens, but in spite of everything still trusts and loves his friend? When we really trust another, we know that even if we do not understand why an incident occurs, we believe in our friend because we know that he was acting in our best interest.

A minister once had a friend who told him that he should not form a fast relationship with a certain person. He said, "I cannot tell you why, but you must not do it and you will just have to trust me." Well, trust him he did, for he knew that his friend was acting in his best interest and had reasons which he could not divulge.

Robert Hall puts it like this: "A friend should be one in whose understanding and virtue we can equally confide, and whose opinion we can value at once for its justness and its sincerity."

Now there are many questions which we cannot answer about God and his world. Many things happen to us which may seem unjust; many sorrows, hard to bear, come our way; many disappointments overtake us unexpectedly along the way. At times we are prone to blame God. "Why did this have to happen to me?" we cry out in our anguish. "Why hast thou forsaken me?" we may utter.

We believe that though we are not freed completely from trouble, yet we are saved in trouble. In other words God offers help in seeing us through. Paul puts it like this in Rom. 8:28 (R.S.V.): "We know that in everything God works for good with those who love him." This tells the sufferer, as Georgia Harkness put it, of the abundant and unfailing resources of God for mastering his pain—a sense of divine concern, confidence that in the midst of it all there is a good to be found which, with the help of God, can lead to richer and deeper living. . . . There is no assurance that to love God will ever pay dividends in freedom from pain; there is every assurance in the Christian gospel that God will find a way to work for good in the worst situations with those who love him and stay their lives upon him.

But with Paul we need to live so close to Christ that we are able to say, "For me to live is Christ." And with Christ we need to say, "Not my will, but thine, be done."

Let us take this lesson from Paul and emulate his faith by placing in God a confidence so great that he does not have to explain his actions, that regardless of what may happen to us we still love and trust him and are able to say: "I know whom I have believed, and am persuaded that he is able to keep that which I have committed unto him against that day."

AIDS TO WORSHIP

Hymns: "My Jesus, as Thou Wilt!"
"Blessed Assurance, Jesus Is Mine!"
Scripture: II Tim. 1:1-14

A Prayer

Most gracious God, whose greatness is beyond the conception of man, we pause today to acknowledge our unworthiness. Judge us, we pray, by thy great mercy and not according to our merits. Coming into thy holy presence makes us conscious of our feebleness and sinfulness, for in thy light our lives are blighted with scars. Yet we would remember the promise of thy Son who assured forgiveness to them who repent and return unto thee.

> Forgive us for doubting moments when thy promises lie hidden in our minds;
> Forgive us of selfish ambitions unbecoming servants of thine;
> Forgive us of jealousies which canker the soul;
> Forgive us for lack of faith when darkness makes us afraid;
> Forgive us for slowness to see the virtues of others and quickness to see their faults.

Stab us awake to our manifold needs. Drive us to our knees in penitence for all our failures and raise us up new servants of thine, through Jesus Christ our Lord. AMEN.

15

2
The church's hidden secret

THE MORE WE STUDY THE CHRISTIAN CHURCH, THE
more profoundly impressed we become with its greatness.
As faulty as it sometimes is and as ineffective as its witness
often becomes, yet we see in it, silently and purposefully
at work, a divine Element.

Outwardly we look upon a building, an organization, a
doctrine, a set of beliefs, a group of people. We see it at
work on Sundays and during the week. There are services
of worship, classes of instruction, periods of fellowship in
social life. There is a missionary outreach. There is social
service in the community. Through it we see Boy and Girl
Scout groups at work, men's clubs, women's groups. Music
occupies an important part of its work as choirs are
trained and lovely music enjoyed.

According to denominations there are policies of operation, a way of doing things. Some are connectional in
nature, each a part of a great movement and organization,
linked together in districts, conferences, jurisdictions.
Others are independent in nature, with each church being
a separate entity having loose connection with others of
like mind.

Outwardly again we observe, as the late Dean Sperry of
Harvard has well said, that "the world seeks the church,

uncritically, habitually at those times when life matters most." He continues by saying:

Parents who have drifted away from the church still bring their children back for baptism. Young people who profess to have outgrown religion still enter the church to be made man and wife. The last low whispers of the world's dead are not uniformly burdened with God's name but the church is always requisitioned to speak that name over those dead. In obedience to some deep unreasoned prompting men seek churches when life is most real.

Now the question, of course, is just why does the church mean so much when life matters most? Why do men turn to it at those times when life is most real?

This can be answered in many ways, but the real secret is that at the heart of the church God, through Christ, reaches out to us in redemptive love. It is more than our doctrine. It is more than our classes and our study. It is more than our organization.

So men come to church when life is most real, for they know that here God makes himself known, that he reaches out to us. As James S. Stewart has put it, "Apostolic Christianity is never merely familiarity with the facts, but always union with the risen Christ." This is the church's hidden secret. When we see only the outward form and activity of the church, we miss that which propels

17

it and which gives it life and which draws men back again and again to it.

Dr. Stewart reminds us that Gibbon missed this when in his *Decline and Fall of the Roman Empire* he attributed the victory of Christianity to five reasons. He said they were "Christian enthusiasm, belief in immortality, miracles, ethics, and organization." But the one decisive factor he omitted was the Presence in the proclamation of the living Christ.

In other words, Stewart is saying here that when we give our testimony to what Christ has done for us that it is not simply human testimony, but the self-testimony of the risen Jesus. When, in our churches, we tell the old, old story, it is more than the relation of a tale; Christ is really speaking through us and is present in our midst.

Yes, the church's hidden secret is the fact that Christ reaches out to us in suffering love, that when we truly seek him, he grips us. Ralph W. Sockman puts it like this: "When we receive Christ into the surrendered will, the open mind, and the loving heart, then the God for whom we have been groping becomes the God who grips us."

Some years ago a man was speaking before a college audience about his religious experience. He told of being taken, as a little lad, by his father on a visit to New York City. To keep from getting lost in the crowd he held to his father's finger. But after a while his little legs grew

tired, his fingers began to lose their grip, and he looked up at his father and said, "You'll have to take hold of my hand now, for I can't hold on much longer."

So this is the reason men come to church; for they feel that when they can't hold on much longer, God is there to hold them and to save them. Thus, the church's hidden secret is that here we find God and God finds us and grips us.

AIDS TO WORSHIP

Hymns: "The Church's One Foundation"
"My Hope Is Built on Nothing Less"
Scripture: John 14:5-21

A PRAYER

Eternal God, from whom cometh every good and perfect gift, we praise thee, we worship thee, we give thanks unto thee for thy great love which is constant and whose concern encompasses all men. On every hand thou dost seek to make thyself known unto us. Open our minds and hearts to thy companionship. Free us from our occupation with the cares of this world and the call of the market place, that we may hear thy still, small voice.

> Breathe into our disordered lives a portion of thy peace.
> Reassure us of thy love as we face the uncertainties of tomorrow.
> Undergird us with thy strength as we walk our feeble ways.

19

Lighten our pathway with thy truth as we face difficult decisions.
Inspire us with thy presence and make us know we labor not alone.

Send us out with the power to do thy will, through Jesus Christ our Lord. AMEN.

20

3
You can count on me

THE OTHER DAY ONE MAN SAID OF ANOTHER, "NOW, he is a good fellow, but you can't count on him to work. He will take the job but will do nothing with it."

This is one trouble with the world today—people who do not carry their own weight in the world's work; people who do not feel that they have a part to play; people who do not play their part when given one.

There are competent folk who never volunteer or permit themselves to be drafted for jobs that need to be done. They readily agree that what is proposed is good, but they always end by saying, "Of course, I can't do it."

A boy from the Middle West who had never seen the ocean stood one day with a friend and looked out across the vast Pacific. Breaking the silence, his friend finally said, "Well, what do you think of it? Don't you think it is wonderful?" "Yes," replied the boy, "but I hate to see all that water out there doing nothing."

So it is with scores of people in every community—people who can and who won't; people who should and who don't; people who take from life and never give.

A minister saw a certificate of membership in some organization hanging on the wall of a friend's office.

Across the top of it were these words, "A Voting Membership." This is the only kind of membership that's really worth while. Voting members are the only ones that count in the affairs of men.

But let us think also of those people who accept jobs and never fulfill them, who take places of responsibility and regard them lightly, who want their names on the list and who do nothing to deserve their being there.

Every church has listed on its official rolls men who have no right by virtue of their labor to be there. The work of the deacons, the vestry, the stewards suffer by indifferent men who take their jobs lightly.

How can self-respecting men continue to let their names appear on boards, committees, and commissions and then absent themselves from all meetings and neglect their share of the load!

Dependability is one of the finest virtues a man or woman can possess. Frequently when asked about the qualifications of young men and women for certain jobs, the first question the employer wants to know is, "Can he or she be depended upon?"

But thank God for men who see what needs to be done and are willing to do it, who give and ask nothing in return. How grateful we should be for those public-spirited citizens who labor that the world and their own community might be a better place in which to live!

All of us have been greatly impressed by men and women who give so unstintingly of their time, effort, and means that ours might be a finer community. We are all indebted to them. Many of them spend hours and hours, out of an interest of genuine concern, in the things that make for better living. These we salute, and may their tribe increase!

AIDS TO WORSHIP

Hymns: "A Charge to Keep I Have"
"Hark, the Voice of Jesus Calling"
Scripture: Rom. 12

A Prayer

Eternal God, who art concerned with all thy children and whose purposes for our lives art always good, in our gratitude for the favors thou dost send our way, let us not be unmindful of the needs of others.

Give us concerned hearts for the hungry, the sick the suffering.
Out of our bounty move us to give to the needy.
In our comfort stir us to share with the burdened.
Use us to bring cheer to little children.
Through us send hope to the discouraged.
We would pray, O God, this day:
For the sick of body and the weary of mind;
For those weighted down with the guilt of sin;
For all who are living in fear and anxiety; and

23

For the sorrowful who listen for steps which will never return.

Give to all weary travelers today strength for the road ahead. In the name of him who came to help men carry life's loads, we pray. AMEN.

24

4
A hitching post or a guidepost?

LESLIE WEATHERHEAD, IN HIS BOOK, "WHEN THE LAMP FLICKERS," has a sentence which reads: "He does not wave to us from the past; He beckons us from the future." Of course this does not intend to minimize the importance of the historical setting out of which Christianity arose. It is firmly established historically and geographically. Our faith is grounded not on myth, but on fact and history.

To say, however, that Jesus does not wave to us from the past but beckons to us from the future is to say that not only is he a historical person who moved across the stage of history, saying and doing wonderful things, setting mankind a marvelous example to follow, and then ascending into heaven; but that Christianity is not a hitching post which holds down, but rather a guidepost pointing the way. It is a faith which has to do with the present and the future.

You remember Jesus' words in the last verse of the last chapter of Matthew when he said, "And, lo, I am with you alway, even unto the end of the world." This is the central fact of our faith and one which needs re-emphasizing in our time—the availability of Christ for today. He is alive and moving and living among us. We do not worship a dead Christ, one that can be kept in a tomb. He escapes every prison house.

In Lloyd Douglas' novel *The Robe*, Marcellus, the converted Roman centurion, had watched the stoning of Stephen. As death came to the first Christian martyr, Stephen raised himself on one arm and shouted triumphantly, "I see him! I see him! My Lord Jesus—take me!" Then his eyes closed and he crumpled in death upon the stones. Marcellus looked into the eyes of a soldier near by.

"That was a strange thing, sir!" muttered the soldier.

"More strange than you think!" exclaimed Marcellus.

"I would have sworn the Greek was dead! He thought he saw someone coming to rescue him!"

"He *did* see someone coming to rescue him!" shouted Marcellus, ecstatically.

"That dead Galilean, maybe?" queried the legionary, nervously.

"That Galilean is not dead, my friend!" declared Marcellus. "He is more alive than any man here!"

Yes, our faith is not a hitching post which ties him down, which anchors him in a tomb, which buries him in a book. It is a guidepost declaring the living reality of our Lord, offering his Presence to walk through life's joys and sorrows with us. Jesus does not wave to us from the past; he beckons to us from the future. He is alive forevermore.

And the greatest assurance we have of life after death

rests in Jesus' word when he said, "Because I live, ye shall live also."

We are like the little dog who went with his master to visit a sick friend. The dog was left outside. Presently, wanting "in," he began to scratch on the door. The sick man asked, "Why does he want to come in here? How does he know it is safe to be in here?" The owner of the dog replied, "Well, you see, he knows his master came through that door; and though he does not know what this room is like, because his master is here he is willing to come in." Is not the same thing true with Christians? We do not know what the other room is like, but because the Master went through it, it takes away some of the fear for us.

Christianity is not a hitching post which ties us to the ashes and dust of this world but rather a guidepost pointing the way and bringing us assurance of our eternal home. Jesus does not wave to us from the past but beckons to us from the future—this is our faith!

AIDS TO WORSHIP

Hymns: "I Know that My Redeemer Lives"
"Saviour, Like a Shepherd Lead Us"
Scripture: Matt. 28:16-20

A PRAYER

Eternal God, thou who has loved us into life and dost love

us through life into life eternal, once again we pause seeking thy ear and listening for thy voice.

We are continually overwhelmed at thy majesty and greatness and yet humbled in gratitude for thy personal concern in our lives. Nothing escapes thy notice, nor is foreign to thy understanding. Thou dost listen, as a father to a child, to our every prayer. Every detail of our lives is of interest to thee. What would we do, O God, without thy love, without thy courage, without thy strength, without thy comfort?

Steady those who are faced with uncertainty. Awaken those who find life drab and colorless. Give us courage to stand for truth, to say no when it is so easy to say yes, to be true to the highest we know. Help us to walk as children of thine. In Christ's name we pray. AMEN.

28

5
As his custom was

IN THE SIXTEENTH VERSE OF THE FOURTH CHAPTER OF
Luke we read these words: "And he came to Nazareth,
where he had been brought up; and he went to the synagogue, as his custom was, on the sabbath day. And he
stood up to read." (R.S.V.) This is the verse we think
of when we turn our thoughts to church worship on Sunday, for here we find an example set by our Lord that we
as Christians are supposed to follow.

The four words found in the middle of this verse immediately catch our attention—"as his custom was." These
words appear only twice in Luke, the other being in the
thirty-ninth verse of the twenty-second chapter of Luke—
and coming near the end of Jesus' earthly life—when he
"went, as was his custom, to the Mount of Olives"
(R.S.V.). It is interesting to note that both times these
words relate to his custom of prayer. Jesus prayed instinc-
tively and habitually, both in company with God's people
and in the solitary hours of his own communion.

Here in this little town of Nazareth, made up of ordi-
nary people, Jesus returned to worship. Why did he do it
here? Certainly the little synagogue was not impressive.
The people were simple folk. And no doubt in many ways

the service was not inspiring. Nevertheless, Jesus was there when the sabbath day came. Why?

Perhaps, for one thing, he knew the value of the association of time and place in one's worship, for it was here he had worshiped as a boy. In such an association the approach to God seems more sure. We are all creatures of associations. Time and place make a difference in how we feel and what we experience.

Now, of course, there are those who say that God is just as real to them out in the wide-open spaces—by the seaside, on the golf course, on top of a mountain—as he is in church, and sometimes even more so. "Why cannot God be found as real with people playing and going places as he is with people in church?" they often argue. Surely, we must answer them that theoretically God might be just as real to some in such varied places, but practically he is not.

To be sure Jesus found God down by the seaside, out on the Sea of Galilee, upon the Mount of Beatitudes, out under the silent stars, down by a spring, on the banks of the river Jordan; but he knew God in these places because he had first found him in the temple, among God's people, in a place which had been dedicated to the worship of God. He found the Father everywhere, because he had first known him somewhere. So, as his custom was, Jesus entered the synagogue on the sabbath day, to find him again in company with God's people.

30

Then, too, Jesus knew the value of linking the present with the past, and this he did in the synagogue. Worship in the temple not only linked him with the present, with people now, and events of everyday life, but it also put him in touch with Israel's long yesterdays. What he was doing every sabbath in the synagogue were not isolated moments of worship but part of the dreams and hopes and aspirations of the generations past. He felt a close tie of kinship with the faith of his fathers.

Jesus knew also the great strength which comes with fellowship in the synagogue. He knew how lonely isolation could be, and how the prayers of the isolated moments could be strengthened by such worship in company with others. It was this corporate worship which added warmth to his soul and helped him feel that he belonged to a group who were traveling the same road as was he.

So Jesus gave silent and steady testimony when he went "as his custom was" to the synagogue on the sabbath day.

To those who take worship on Sundays lightly and in their complacency imagine that they have no real need for it, let them look at the Son of man and his stated need, and let his custom be for them a rebuke. For if he needed it, how much more do we!

> Dear Lord and Father of mankind!
> Forgive our foolish ways!
> Reclothe us in our rightful mind,

31

In purer lives Thy service find,
In deeper reverence, praise.

. . . .

Drop Thy still dews of quietness,
Till all our strivings cease;
Take from our souls the strain and stress,
And let our ordered lives confess
The beauty of Thy peace.
—JOHN GREENLEAF WHITTIER

AIDS TO WORSHIP

Hymns: "Safely Through Another Week"
"From All that Dwell Below the Skies"
Scripture: Luke 4:16-20

A PRAYER

Almighty God, giver of every good and perfect gift, to thee
we lift our praise and thanksgiving. On every hand we see thy
mercy and love expressed. Thy world with all its bounty and
loveliness is a creation of thy hand. Our lives with all their
possibilities were fashioned by thee. Thou hast made it all
and declared it good.

Wherever we see thy creation distorted we know it is
partly man's sin which has caused it. Wherever men are in
want it is not thy will, for there is enough and to spare in
thy world. Wherever men are dying through mortal conflict
thy will for them is being denied. Forgive us, O holy One,
for our manifold sins. Judge us not according to our merits,
but in thy great love and mercy toward us.

Send us forth to live at our best, through Jesus Christ our
Lord. AMEN.

32

6
Worry—wrecker of life

THERE IS A STORY TOLD OF TWO MEN VACATIONING AT the beach. One was depressed and planned to end it all. The other said, "Let's sit down and talk it over." They did and after thirty minutes both jumped in. The despondency of one man and its contagious influence on the other is symptomatic of the worry and fear which stalk the earth today. Worry wrecks more lives than wars. Let us see what it does to life.

In the first place, worry is a wrecker of life. It is a destroyer of happiness. Life for most people would be happy and satisfying if they could overcome worry. In a real sense worry is the interest you pay on trouble before it comes—and many times it never comes.

All of us have had the experience of fretting over something we were afraid would happen, only to find that it never happened. We have crossed bridges before we got to them and often have discovered that there were no bridges to cross. As a wrecker of life worry not only destroys happiness but is a breaker of health. We are told that one out of ten people in the United States will have a nervous breakdown, and many of these breakdowns will be caused by worry and emotional conflicts.

Dr. O. F. Gober, the late chief physician of the Santa

Fe Hospital Association, once said: "Seventy per cent of all patients who come to physicians could cure themselves if they only got rid of their fears and worries."

Again, as a wrecker of life worry incapacitates us for work. All of us have had the experience of being worried, and we know how it slows us down in our work because our minds are otherwise engaged. In a real sense men don't work themselves into graves; they worry themselves into them.

The big question, then, is how are we to handle our worries, how can we overcome them? Someone has well said, "All the constitution guarantees is the pursuit of happiness. You have to catch up with it for yourself."

For one thing, it is good to ask just why we are worrying. Get all the facts. What is the origin of the worry? Where did it come from? Is it real or imaginary? Many times we discover that to run worries down often leads to their disappearance. We shake the bear and find it to be a bush. Worry frequently is fear of failure, a concern lest we fail to measure up to what is expected of us. We worry about what people will say.

Not only does it help to get the facts, but then we should do something about them. Our worries should be met with action. Dr. Abraham Myerson, a psychologist, strongly insists on action—even if it is unwise action—for such is better than living under fear which tends to breed indecision. Brooding is the worst thing we can do.

And then, let us try to live one day at a time. Do the job at hand. To worry over what must be done next year, to add up all that one week demands—such is enough to make us worry. But if we meet well today's task, the hour's responsibility, then chances are we will be ready for next week's demands.

Finally, the greatest antidote for worry is to commit life each day into the hands of a loving and kind God. Such trust banishes worry; strong faith drives it out. Take verses such as these into your daily round and worry will be crowded out: "In quietness and in confidence shall be [my] strength." "I can do all things through Christ which strengtheneth me." "The Lord is my shepherd; I shall not want."

This trust will bring inner peace. Alexis Carrel put it like this: "Those who keep the peace of their inner selves in the midst of the tumult of the modern city are immune from nervous diseases." In any event we know that a strong faith and trust in God brings peace of mind and drives out worry.

AIDS TO WORSHIP

Hymns: "How Firm a Foundation"
            "God Is My Strong Salvation"
Scripture: Ps. 23

A Prayer

Eternal God, creator of all life, ruler of all nature, source of all strength, we give thanks unto thee for thy great love toward us and toward all men. Into thy holy presence we come, lifting our common supplications unto thee. Thou knowest the needs of our hearts—our fears, our anxieties, our unanswered perplexities. The burdens we carry are known by thee. The heartaches which disturb us are not foreign to thy knowledge.

> Keep us still that we may listen.
> Keep us believing that we may know.
> Keep us pure that we may see.
> Keep us brave that we may venture.
> Keep us close that we may walk in confidence.

Send us out, O God, with assurance that life with all its fears can be faced in victory with thee. AMEN.

1
You are welcome at church

MANY CHURCHES ARE FREQUENTLY ENGAGED IN PRO-
grams of visitation evangelism in which church members
go out two by two to see people for the church in the
name of Christ.

There are several reflections which come from such
programs. For one thing, it is a rich experience for those
who visit in the name of Christ. They come back with
reports of victory and the joy which has been theirs in
this service. Their mission is not one of asking for money
but, rather, one of witnessing to the joy of the Christian
faith and of inviting others to accept this faith.

Again, it brings into the church people who need such
a fellowship and who need the assurances of the Christian
faith. In short, it attempts to introduce men to Christ as
Lord of life and leader of men. And how we all need to
know him!

Sherwood Eddy puts it like this: "It is our conviction
that what we need most today is not the priceless privilege
of the early twelve to see and know the historic Jesus, but
rather the experience of Christ which transformed Saul
into Paul and created the early church."

Ministers of all denominations agree that most people
are reached today by such a personal approach. The

37

church must go out and seek the lost and bring them in. But there is another reflection that must be mentioned which concerns a lot of people. This is the responsibility of those who at one time or another accepted Christ and united with his church. It is the responsibility which should rest heavily upon those who are members of the church to be active in the church.

Some time ago, a minister said, "I am greatly concerned with the attitude of so many people who move into a new community and who assume that the Church should look them up. If they are true to their vows, they will look the Church up."

How right he is! Every church member who leaves one community and goes to another should make himself or herself known at some church. The school does not seek out the children; the parents take their children to the school. So should they take their children to some church school as well as themselves.

Now, of course, the church must be concerned in those who are outside or who have lost interest in it. A lot of people expect too much of the church in this "hide-and-go-seek game." Part of moving a family to a new community is moving that family to a house of worship as well as to a school of public education. Sometimes parents say, "Nobody has been to see me from any church since we moved here." The real question should be, "Have they been to a church and made themselves known as new residents of the community?"

The answer then of course is twofold: church people should seek to find the church as well as the church seeking to find them.

Surely every church in most communities warmly welcomes new people whose presence adds so much to its fellowship, but every church member should help by presenting himself at church.

Someone wrote this:

The Church is a lighthouse . . . In a dark world it keeps alive the flame of truth and love and righteousness. It sheds the light of Christian virtues across the pathway of humanity.

The Church is a powerhouse . . . It does not create power, but it transmits power. It puts men in contact with that source of all power which is God.

The Church is a citadel . . . It stands like a rock against those forces which strive to profane the name of God, and which plot and scheme to cause men to forsake God.

The Church is a hospice . . . It is a house by the side of the road, giving succor to the heartsick and afflicted, lifting the fallen and protecting the defenseless.

You are welcome at church!

AIDS TO WORSHIP

Hymns: "Come, Ye that Love the Lord"
"Blest Be the Tie that Binds"
Scripture: Acts 2:41-47

A Prayer

O merciful God, companion of men's souls, strength of men's wills, comforter of men's sorrows, what would we do without thee! O gracious One:

> When we are lonely, thou art near;
>
> When we are afraid, thou dost reassure us;
>
> When we are tempted, thou dost reinforce us;
>
> When we are in far places, thou dost unite us in spirit with those we love;
>
> When men fail us, thou dost hold our faith in what they can become;
>
> When anxiety grips our inmost being, thou dost bring inner peace and calm;
>
> When we flee from thee in sinful living, thou dost still tug at our hearts;
>
> When we come back to thee, thou dost open thine arms in forgiveness and receive us back unto thyself again;
>
> When life's end stares us in the face, thou art one who dost open the door into thy eternal home.

For thy presence, thy comfort, thy strength, thy power, thy forgiveness, we give thee our heart's gratitude. In the name of him who is our Lord we pray. AMEN.

8
Sheep still need a shepherd

SEVERAL SUMMERS AGO A MINISTER WAS IN SOUTH
Dakota visiting friends who owned a sheep ranch. They
took him one day out across the range where the sheep
were grazing. As he left this pastoral scene, knowing that
sheep still need a shepherd, he thought of David's twenty-
third psalm where David likens people to sheep and the
Lord to a shepherd.

It was but natural that David would use such figures
of speech and natural, too, that Jesus would use the figure
of a shepherd's care in watching over his sheep in speaking
of God's love and care for his children.

This shepherd's psalm has "dried many a tear and sup-
plied the mold into which many hearts have poured their
faith." It is the utterance of personal trust in the Lord,
darkened by no fears or complaints, asking for nothing
but grateful for such care.

In this psalm of quiet trust the one central thought is
expanded in two kindred images—that of the *shepherd*
and of the *host*.

In the first image, God sustains us. He is our guide on
the journey of life. "The Lord is my shepherd." How
much meaning is packed into those melodious words! We

41

see him as our guide protecting us from evil and harm.

Even if "I walk through the valley of the shadow of death[or gloom], I will fear no evil: for thou art with me; thy rod and thy staff they comfort me." The valley of the shadow is not necessarily death, but moments of darkness and despair, hours of loneliness and disappointment. But even in death we are never alone. God is with us; his rod and his staff are our stays. To the sheep out in the wilderness, the shepherd and his staff protect them from harm.

So the journey of life is not always bright and smooth, but sometimes plunges us down into grim canyons where no sunbeams reach. Even so, that anticipation can be met with calm. "Thou art with me" is enough.

The second image we have is that of host. God not only sustains us; he entertains us. We are really guests of God enjoying his hospitality. He even gives us a banquet "in the presence of mine enemies." Or, as the Book of Common Prayer has it, "in the presence of them that trouble me."

"The Lord is my shepherd; I shall not want. He maketh me to lie down in green pastures: he leadeth me beside the still waters." Here the Psalmist tells of the tender care of God for childhood, when we are only lambs. A lamb is too timid to drink of rough waters. Thus, "he leadeth me beside still waters." "Goodness and mercy" follow us all the way until at last we are in the Father's house.

Then we find the spirit of Jesus in the psalm. Listen to his words: "I am the good shepherd: the good shepherd giveth his life for the sheep"; "My sheep hear my voice, and I know them, and they follow me."

For us Jesus Christ is the Good Shepherd. He is the one who follows us through thick and thin. His spirit is let loose in the world. He is alive forevermore. We see him going in search of the lost sheep, yearning for each one to be in the Father's fold.

Indeed, "The Lord is my shepherd!"

AIDS TO WORSHIP

Hymns: "The Lord Is My Shepherd"
       "Saviour, Like a Shepherd Lead Us"
Scripture: Ps. 23

A Prayer

Eternal God, in whom there is no darkness, and from whom we find light for life's journey, with gratitude we come into thy holy presence this day. We cannot fully know thee or completely understand thee; yet what we know inspires us to love and worship thee.

We rejoice that thou hast made thyself known to us through thy Son, Jesus Christ our Lord. Help us to find in him today, through the Holy Spirit, strength and power for our feeble lives. We rejoice that every event of our mortal lives is watched of thee. We know that nothing escapes thy notice. Renew within our hearts the faith that all things work together for good to them that love thee.

43

Grant to every one of us this day the help and strength we need. Fill our fearful lives with confident trust. Quicken our faltering steps to a steady pace. Flood our sorrowful hearts with abiding joy and lift our lonely souls with thy comforting presence, through Christ our Lord. AMEN.

9
Doing the best
with what you have

MANY THERE ARE TODAY WHO ARE LIVING WITH IN-
ward discord brought about by a tension between what
they are and what they long to be. Each one of us has
faced a situation where on one side are aligned things
as they are—our capacities, our abilities—and on the other
what we are hoping they will eventually be. On the one
hand is the actual self and on the other the vision of the
ideal. Oftentimes the gap between these two positions is
so great that inwardly we feel frustrated. Dreams become
too lofty ever to have a chance of being achieved. One
study of 275 college students revealed that 90 per cent
of them suffered from a haunting feeling of deficiency.

Now to be sure it is good to have dreams of the person
you hope to become, but to dream too high is oftentimes
as dangerous as to dream too low. When what we are and
what we hope to be face each other with no chance of
meeting, then an inward civil war begins.

This may sound rather strange to be cautioning anyone
to watch the heights of his ambition, for so many are
dreaming too low today. Many never aspire to greatness
but drift along in the lazy bays, going with the current.

Surely the world needs men and women who dare to aspire, to dream, to look upward. But to dream too high may become in itself self-defeating when the summit is never approached. To hold high ambitions is a man's glory, and a vital part of it is in the development of personality, but this happy faculty, if misdirected, can tear life to pieces.

As we face this matter of starting with life as it is, we find that we must accept ourselves. We must face frankly our abilities as well as the limitations which life has given us.

This principle of self-acceptance can be applied in every realm of life. A peach tree will not produce apples. Tomatoes will not bear from beans or corn. These things were not intended to produce other than what they are. Of course botanists can perform wonders in grafting and cross breeding, but the major functions of plant life remain the same.

So, in these lives of ours God does not intend for us to do the impossible. And just because one can become an eminent physician does not mean that he is fulfilling a greater function in the eyes of God than one who, through his mechanical mind, brings forth an electric light. An Edison is no less important to the world than a Mayo. The same thing holds true as far as our varied abilities are concerned. Some can do many things and do them well; others can do only a few, or perhaps one thing well.

In a fascinating biography of one of America's greatest sons, *George Washington Carver*, by Rackham Holt, there is a little poem written by Carver in his youth that fits our thought here. One verse goes like this:

> O! sit not down nor idly stand;
> There's plenty to do on every hand.
> If you cannot prosper in work like some,
> You've at least one talent, improve that one.[1]

Surely this is all that God requires of us, to do the best we can with what we have. And it is said of Carver that "one by one the things he could not do well were being pruned away, to leave the things he could do supremely well."

No one has had a more undesirable beginning than George Washington Carver, who just before his death was called one of the world's greatest agricultural chemists. He was born in a slave home, stolen by slave thieves, and taken to live in a white man's home without mother or father. He was equipped with a frail body. Yet from such a start he rose to a place of fame and was the recipient of hundreds of honors. This great man, whose picture now adorns one of our postage stamps, surely had to start with life's remainders, but he did the best he could with what he had.

---

[1] Used by permission of Doubleday & Company, Inc.

What are you doing with what you have? This is the most important question we face today. The little boy on the hillside had only five loaves and two fish, but they fed the multitude. With them alone he could do little, but in co-operation with Christ wonders were achieved. The world is full of life's noblemen who have traveled far on little baggage—not only people who gain fame, but humble folk whose name will never be recorded in the annals of history but will be written indelibly in God's book of life.

And it is never too late to start over again. In A. J. Cronin's book, *Keys of the Kingdom,* the Chinese gardener Fu was distressed over what a storm did to his flowers. But Father Chisholm said: "Let us be of good cheer, Fu. The damage is not irreparable." "My plantings are lost," Fu gloomily replied. "We shall have to begin all over again." Then Father Chisholm responded: "That is life . . . to begin again when everything is lost!"

AIDS TO WORSHIP

Hymns: "Lord, Speak to Me, that I May Speak"
"Take My Life, and Let It Be"
Scripture: Prov. 3:1-10

A Prayer

O God, we come to thee empty-handed, for all that we possess cometh from thee. We stand before thee as having nothing except what thou hast provided.

48

We are small, but thou art great;
We are weak, but thou art strong;
We are ignorant, but thou art wise;
We are finite, but thou art infinite;
We are revengeful, but thou art forgiving;
We are sinful, but thou art pure.

O God, how dependent we are upon thee. Thou art our hope, our strength, and our life. AMEN.

10
Lest we forget

IN THE SECOND CHAPTER OF THE BOOK OF DANIEL WE
have the interesting story of how King Nebuchadnezzar
had a dream that troubled him. To add to his trouble he
could not remember what he had dreamed.

We know that Eastern people, and especially the Jews,
had a high regard for dreams and their meaning. They
did not take them lightly, and there were those who pro-
fessed to be able to interpret dreams and their meanings.
We recall the ancient custom among the Egyptians and
remember that it was in Pharaoh's house where such
validity was given to dreams. The whole story is found in
Genesis and deals with the dreams of Pharaoh's butler and
baker and even Pharaoh himself. Here it is that Joseph
plays a great part as an interpreter of dreams.

Now the king was disturbed, for apparently he had forgotten his dream and sought not only answer to its
meaning but also what the dream itself was. He therefore
called the magicians, the astrologers, the sorcerers, and the
Chaldeans.

He told them that he wanted to know what it was he
had dreamed, as well as the answer to it; and if this could
not be forthcoming, he threatened them with destruction.

You recall the story of how they were helpless to answer his inquiry and of how Daniel, a man of God, was called in and saved the day by his interpretation.

But the point of our story today is not what Daniel was able to tell the king, but that many of us have lost our dreams and need to be reminded of them. We have forgotten the dreams of earlier years and need to call them to mind.

Guy O. Carpenter has said that the job of the minister or the preacher is to make the people remember the dreams they have forgotten. In one sense with Nebuchadnezzar we all cry out, "Tell me my dreams and what they mean." But let us now turn to some things that we should remember, some of the dreams we may have forgotten.

First, let us remember who we are. We are human beings. We are members of the human family. We are children of God.

Of course there are those today who speak rather disparagingly of human nature and its importance. Someone has spoken of man as being a sick fly on a dizzy wheel. The materialist refers to him as a bundle of electrons without a soul, and some psychologists—certainly no Christian ones—would have us believe that man is merely a jumble of stimuli-response reactions with no enduring value.

So, in the face of such low views of man we need to

51

remind ourselves of our heritage. We are creatures of importance because we are important to God.

In I John 3:1 we have these words: "Behold, what manner of love the Father hath bestowed upon us, that we should be called the sons of God." Indeed, behold such love. Remember it. Fasten your mind upon it.

Second, let us remember not only who we are but where we are headed. We are headed somewhere as human beings. One thing Moses did for the children of Israel was to give them a sense of importance and purpose. We are on a journey; we are headed for eternity.

Today we need to remember the Eternal in the light of the present. To see life against a divine background gives new and added meaning to it.

Third, let us remember not only who we are, where we are headed, but also what our rules are. By what are we living? What is our code in life? For what purpose do we live? Who sets the rules and what are they? Do they have the note of permanency about them? Or are they expedient only—serving the moment?

We should not forget the dreams and ideals which were once ours. Every one of us has had moments in life in which we had great dreams for ourselves, for our world, for our church. We dreamed of the person we might become. We dreamed of the person we some day would marry and the Christian home that would be established.

Many of us have forgotten those ideals. We have found ourselves in a world which is not too idealistic, and we have said, "So what, a man must live, he must get along." Most of us have not held fast to the ideals which were once ours.

Our rules as Christians are those set by Jesus Christ our Lord. Let us keep them ever close to us and test all our living by them.

Finally, let us remember who we are, where we are headed, what our rules are, and who our pilot is. It is not enough merely to remember our heritage, our destination, the rules of the course; we need more than anything else in the world to remember Jesus Christ. He is our pilot.

This is what Paul told his young friend Timothy. Even if he forgot everything else he told him, this one thing he wanted him never to forget, "Remember Jesus Christ."

What a different world this would be if more people remembered him today! What different people you and I would be if within our life and memory he reigned supreme—this matchless teacher; this great character; this man in whom God breathed and whom God called his Son!

Joseph Sizoo tells of a man who said that the world was done with Jesus Christ. But the answer given was this: "No, the world is done without him." And so are we.

53

AIDS TO WORSHIP

Hymns: "Christ's Life Our Code"
"Dear Master, in Whose Life I See"
Scripture: I John 3:1-11

A PRAYER

Eternal God, whose greatness and majesty are beyond the reaches of our highest thoughts and yet who art within the hearts of each one of us, we lift our voices in praise and adoration to thee. No interest of our lives escapes thy notice. No joy is foreign to thy understanding. No thought or motive is unknown to thee. Our lives stand before thee as open books. So, today we lay bare our hearts and minds asking that thou wouldst cleanse them with thy goodness.

Into thy presence we come, conscious of our sins and shortcomings. So much have we done which we ought not to have done, and so much have we left undone that we ought to have done, that there is little health in us. But we come not as those who have no hope, nor as those who can only drown in their sins, for in thee do we find new life and forgiveness, new chances and beginnings. Take us as we are and make us over, we pray, through Jesus Christ our Lord. AMEN.

Now is the time

ONE OF THE GREATEST CHRISTIAN LEADERS OF THE early church, Augustine, once said, "Man lives by the tradition of the past, in the hope of the future, but makes his decisions in the present." No truer statement has ever been made concerning the life of man, and it is especially appropriate in this hour of world's history.

We cannot possibly separate ourselves from the past, the future, or the present. The life we live today is related to that of yesterday and determines that of tomorrow.

Let us look at the phrase "man lives by the tradition of the past." We certainly cannot separate ourselves from that which has gone before. To a great extent we are products of the past not only in biological inheritance but in social inheritance. We are but the lengthened shadows of our forebears. We benefit by the experience of men through the ages, and foolish is the man who refuses to listen to what history can teach him.

But tradition becomes a millstone when we not only accept it as a background but refuse to move out from it into the present and future. There are those who are living today on the religious experience of their forebears. They have not found God for themselves, but all these years have been dependent upon mother's, father's, or grandmother's religious experience. To depend upon another's religious experience is no more satisfying than to depend upon the food that another eats. The past is a hindrance when it is continually referred to as a substitute for the present. You have undoubtedly been to a city or village which seemed to be living only in the past, one which reveled in its tradition and was existing only in the memory of it.

It is not enough to "live in the tradition of the past"; we must live "in the hope of the future." Augustine means by this that man must always have his eyes pointed to "out-there, the is-to-be." We, to be sure, cannot live in the present unless we have our eyes pointed to the future. In the future there is always hope. Even when hope has faded from this earthly realm, there is the hope of the future grounded in a good and kind God.

But to live in the tradition of the past and in the hope of the future is not enough, for as Augustine said, we "make our decisions in the present." This is the whole crux of the matter. Decisions must be made now. There are too many who are looking backward at those made in the past or to the future to those that will be made then. Now is the time!

In Josh. 24:15 we find these words: "And if it seem evil unto you to serve the Lord, choose you this day whom ye will serve." This note of urgency needs so to be struck today. Now is the time! Choose you this day whom ye shall serve.

In this verse we can see how Joshua was challenging his people with a loyalty to Johovah, their God. He was making the matter urgent. Choose you this day, he was saying. It is not enough to look backward to the day your parents were loyal to God or even when you first made your covenant with him. Nor is it enough to look to tomorrow for your fidelity to him; but, rather, now is the time.

Now is the time for us to decide what we shall do with Jesus the Christ. We see him standing there at the head of the column of mankind. Shall we dare follow him? There are many today with good intentions who say, "Maybe tomorrow I will decide." They are like Augustine who before his conversion prayed, "Give me purity, O Lord, but not just now." But time ticks on and no man knows what the morrow has in store for him. There are great decisions every human soul should make. We dare not put them off until tomorrow. One decision all must make. Will we or will we not accept the Christ?

In an old legend we find the story of a man walking through an enchanted forest. Suddenly he came upon a sundial and saw on it these words, "It is later than you think." So it is. We must be in haste. Now is the time for us to have dealings with God and to start life afresh— resolve to live a finer, cleaner, nobler life. Yes, "Man lives by the tradition of the past, in the hope of the future, but

57

makes his decision in the present." "Choose you this day whom ye will serve." Now is the time!

AIDS TO WORSHIP

Hymns: "O Jesus, Thou Art Standing"
"Only Trust Him"
Scripture: Josh. 24:14-18

A PRAYER

Eternal God, in whom we live and move and have our being, with thankful hearts we praise thy holy name. This is thy world and we are thy children living in the Father's house. But we bow our heads in shame because we have not lived as kindred one with another. Our selfishness and pride have separated us; our prejudice has divided us. We have not loved one another as thou hast willed that we should. Forgive us for our unbrotherly ways.

We come, too, confessing our sin in thinking too highly of ourselves. We know that we are weak and frail beings in need of a Redeemer and a Saviour who can lift us out of our sordid selves. So, we come to thee today in need of the Christ who is the Saviour of the world and who alone can save us from sin. Take us this day and make us more worthy servants of thine, through Jesus Christ our Lord. AMEN.

12
God's mercy is measureless

AT THE CLOSE OF EVERY WORSHIP SERVICE IT IS THE custom in most churches to conclude with a benediction. They are verses of scripture which ask God's guidance and blessings upon us as we leave. There is one benediction less frequently used than others and yet meaningful and reassuring in its words:

Unto God's gracious mercy and protection we commit you; and the blessing of God Almighty, the Father, the Son, and the Holy Spirit, be upon you, and remain with you always. Amen.

The first part of this benediction seems to sum up in a measure the real meaning of them all. "Unto God's gracious mercy and protection we commit you." Here the blessing of a merciful God is being asked. It is a word that has to do with God's tender compassion, that pity which he has for man in his weakness and misery and helplessness. It speaks of God's generous and kindly disposition.

God's mercy is a free gift. We do not earn it or merit it; it is freely given. Just as an earthly father gives his love to his children whether they merit it or not, so God's love reaches out to his children.

59

Yet, there are a lot of people who feel they can purchase the mercy of God. They want to enter into a commercial transaction with him. They bargain by saying, "O God, if you will let me get well, I'll be a better person." But he is interested in our getting well whether we are better persons or not. We cannot buy his favor.

In fact, our good works may separate us from God in that we make them a substitute for loving and worshiping him. The Scriptures say, "God is a Spirit: and they that worship him must worship him in spirit and in truth." "The Father seeketh such to worship him." But whether we worship him or not, his mercy and tender compassion are around our lives. They are free gifts.

When we pray, "Unto God's gracious mercy and protection we commit you," let us remember that his mercy and protection are meted out to us when we are unaware of it. It is a wonderful thought to believe that God's protection hovers over us when we sleep. We can close our eyes in peaceful slumber knowing that the "everlasting arms of God" uphold us.

He has so made us that when our bodies are injured, immediately there is set up a series of functions that seek to repair the damage. For example, Alexis Carrel writes:

When a limb is broken, the sharp ends of the fractured bones tear muscles and blood vessels. They are soon surrounded by a bloody clot of fibrin. Then, circulation becomes more active. The limb swells. The nutritive substances necessary for the regeneration of the tissues are brought into the wounded area. All processes are directed toward repair.

Wonderful body!

This is God's protection at work when we are unaware of it. And we need not be afraid of the darkness and unknown when we know that God's protection hovers over us.

But this leads us to a third thought about his mercy and grace, namely, that our experience of his mercy is in direct proportion to our sense of felt need. When we rely upon it, depend upon it, and seek it, we feel its power. God's mercy and grace are always about our lives, but to know and feel their power we must open our hearts to them. It is when we are broken in spirit and contrite of heart and seek for help—it is then we know God's power. In Luke 21:28 we have the same truth expressed when Jesus says, "When these things come to pass, then look up, and lift up your heads; for your redemption draweth nigh."

In other words, Jesus is saying here that it is in moments like these—sickness, death, heartaches—that God draws nigh. It is then that "your redemption draweth nigh." What did he mean? He meant that in hours of trouble God comes very close to the human heart.

It is not that God isn't near when all is well; God is

61

always close to us. His mercy is ever about our lives. But we are so conditioned by pain and sorrow that we are ready to receive God's mercy and grace. In other words, we lose confidence in our own strength and adequacy and make ourselves ready to receive the help of God. God cannot do much for us who feel no sense of need, but it is when we are broken in spirit and humble of heart that he can come in and uphold us.

So in our moments of agony and unhappiness and sorrow, let us see them not only as tragic intrusions of unwanted experiences, but also as opportunities for us to come close to God, to feel his strengthening power and his tender compassion.

AIDS TO WORSHIP

Hymns: "Faith of Our Fathers"
"He Leadeth Me"
Scripture: Luke 21:25-33

A PRAYER

O God our Father, in whose hands our lives rest and in whose providence we spend our days, there are so many mysteries that baffle our minds. There are so many questions we cannot answer. There are so many problems to make us doubt. We do not know and understand all we want to know. Our faith is not firm as we want it to be. But, O God, we do know enough of thy goodness, thy forgiveness, thy love to make us want to hold fast to thee. We do know that:

62

Thou hast been so gracious and art one to whom we
  owe life itself;

Thy hand hast been upon our shoulders guiding faltering footsteps;

Thy presence hast surrounded our being, bringing
  comfort in hours of distress;

Thy love hast forgiven our sinful ways offering new
  beginnings; and

Thy strength has upheld us reinforcing our weakness.

Continue, we pray, to illumine our darkness and displace
our doubts with thy assurance. In his name, which is above all
names, we pray. AMEN.

13
Faith is more than belief

MANY TIMES IN RECENT YEARS YOUNG MEN VISITING their homes for the last time before going overseas had in their possession sealed orders. They did not know their destination.

In a real sense we all sail forth each day under sealed orders. We know not what the day may bring forth. Life is quick with mystery.

How shall we meet it—with faith or fear? That is the question. To meet it with fear means failure; it takes all meaning from life, robbing it of joy. To meet it with faith adds hope to life; it gives joy in living.

Such was the faith which led Abraham into the unknown. We read in the Scriptures: "By faith Abraham, when he was called . . . went out, not knowing whither he went." He went by faith. What was that faith?

Faith is more than belief *about* God; it is trust *in* God. Real faith goes deeper than mere belief. We can believe in something—that is, believe that it exists or believe that it is true—without giving ourselves to it. But real faith goes beyond belief to trust. It is an act of the will. To have faith we must have an abiding trust.

Let us contrast the attitudes of two men. Both believe in God; both believe in immortality; both believe in the goodness of God. Both attest to a firm belief. But here is the difference: one has a deep faith, a trust, dependence upon that which he believes to be true. The other lacks this trust. The first, when he is sick, is not fretful. Facing an operation, he does so in trust, in poise, in confidence. The other faces illness as a child. He is frightened; he is fearful. He cannot bear bad news. His belief does not extend to a firm faith which is trust. One faces death with confidence and with hope. He knows him whom he has believed. He rests his life on the "everlasting arms." He trusts his Lord. The other, facing the uncertainty of illness, becomes a man torn with fears. He lacks deep faith.

So to have real faith you must have trust. Faith goes beyond belief to trust. Philosophy deals with belief; religion deals with trust. One is an assent of the mind; the other, an act of the will. Belief is theology; trust is religion. Trust, of course, cannot exist without belief. But when one seeks the inner glory of the religious life there must be trust in a Person. Men do not lay down their lives for abstract theories any more than they would suffer martyrdom, as Chesterton remarked, for the meridian of Greenwich.

It is when belief moves over into trust and dependence that men and women are willing to give their lives in devotion and sacrifice to Christ. It is when belief in ideas becomes trust in a lifelong comrade that missionaries journey into far-off fields.

Jesus sensed this need of men to really trust. When in Luke 12:28 he said, "O ye of little faith!" he seemed to be asking these questions: Do you merely believe in God or do you believe in him enough to give your life to his keeping? Do you believe in his promises enough to trust your life to him in the unknown future? Do you go out each day in confidence? Do you live unafraid knowing that always about your life is everlasting mercy? Do you live a fretful life or one of inner peace?

Jesus knew that faith must operate in stormy weather as well as on sunny days. But too many of us have a fair-weather faith. We believe when all is well, but our beliefs are shaken when trouble comes.

God is good, we reason, when the sun is shining and life is running in gear, but when a storm arises, when a war reaches into our homes and gets our sons, then it is our shallow belief crumbles unless our faith is grounded in a deathless trust.

The only basis for a faith that sustains is trust in the fatherhood of God—a God who cares, who is close to us, who is always there, who always seeks to help us, whose plans for our lives exceed our fondest hopes. On such a living, moving, accessible Being—not merely a belief in, but a deep trust that is willing to risk all in his hands— on such do we have a faith that propels.

What does a faith like that do for us? Radiant lives all

around testify to its fruits. It frees our minds from fears of the future for work with tasks at hand. It sends us out in confidence. It starts us onward into each new day with a sense of adventure—that this is God's world and we are his children working in it for him.

It gives us a sense of mission. We become people with assignments, with jobs to do for him. When a person loses this sense of mission he loses one of the greatest driving forces in life. It frees us from hurried nervousness, a cause for so much illness today. It centers our inner life around one Master and saves us from splitting our lives by trying to go in all directions at once. In short, it becomes for us a saving faith.

AIDS TO WORSHIP

Hymns: "O Love that Wilt Not Let Me Go"
           "There's a Wideness in God's Mercy"
Scripture: Rom. 8:14-28

A Prayer

Eternal God, in whom we live and move and have our being, thou art our refuge and strength. With grateful hearts we praise thee this day. We know that thou art ever near to guard and to guide. Even when we are unaware of thy presence, thy love reaches out to us and blesses us.

Here this day we rest our fears into thy gracious keeping. We know that without thy strength life's loads would be too much for us and life's fears would cause us to stumble. Facing

67

life with thee our moments of uncertainty turn to hours of adventure, and our times of suffering become opportunities for knowing thee better.

Give us this day a clearer grasp of the things which belong unto our peace, through Jesus Christ our Lord. AMEN.

14
Ideals—also power to see them through

EVERY ONE OF US HAS A CODE OF CONDUCT BY WHICH daily life is measured. For some to follow that code has become an unconscious habit; it is indeed part of us. Yet, I am thinking today how often you and I feel that we need something more which will help us follow that which we know to be right.

We know in general what is right, but how hard it is at times to follow the right. Certainly the complexities of modern life have forced us to reduce our religion to something simple to which we may hold. Some time ago, a man stated that his religion was following the Golden Rule, and he thought that was enough. High code? Yes! But do we not need something more which will help us follow that code?

Several years ago a student said he could easily see why the ignorant and superstitious needed a religion, but as for himself, ethics and philosophy were sufficient. Could we not answer him like this: "Yes, to be sure you have a code of conduct, a system of morality, a high set of ideals. But can you give yourself completely to a set of ideals? Yes, you have a code. But what will give you the power

69

to follow that code? You have perhaps gleaned from the ages what man has found to be the best way to live, but what will give you courage and strength needed to live that type of life?"

It is here that religion comes in, for it offers not only a high system of ideals but also a source of strength and power needed to see them through. And when religion is viewed only as a set of ideals, then it becomes a half-truth. When it is watered down to merely a code of ethics or a standard of conduct, then it ceases to become a religion and remains only a formula or a set of rules.

Have you ever felt that your religion was a burden to you, keeping you from enjoying life, and that you would like to throw it overboard? When we feel that way, it means just this—we have a high set of ideals and little or no power to see them through. Ideals without incentive or motivating power are like automobiles without gasoline, lighting fixtures without electricity.

A high sense of duty, yes, but with it a high level of power. For many years so much of our preaching has been centered on the ethics of Jesus—his way of life, his high standards of living—and this has helped to reduce our faith in a large measure to a matter of conduct. We need not only to say "behave" but also "behold"—"Behold the Lamb of God that taketh away the sins of the world." The greatness of Jesus rests not only in his high ethical teachings but more in that power which enabled him to

70

live those teachings—in his power to see them through.

His uniqueness lay in his relationship to God from whence came his power. The way Jesus lived and his principles in life were the result of his close fellowship with the Father. He lived as he did because God gave him the power to do so. Before a hard day or after the cares and problems of the multitude had pressed upon him until nightfall, he would go apart in quiet and meditation to be alone with God. And after each such hour he came back a new man—a man not only with a high sense of duty but also with a high level of power.

How we need this today! In a radio broadcast to the world, the late Archbishop of Canterbury, William Temple, made this statement: "The deepest need of the world is to return to the will of God. 'Thy will be done' must not be a mere aspiration but a call to action."

For too long now we have left God out of the picture. We have forgotten that he is the sovereign ruler of this universe, that he is not only creator but sustainer as well. We have thought for long that we could run our own lives and the affairs of the world without his help. We must return to the God of our fathers.

William James once said, "The more ideals a man has, the more contemptible is he, if the matter ends there, and if there is no courage shown, no privations undergone, no scars contracted in the attempt to get them realized."

Walter Horton says that, "We had better reckon up with

71

what an experience of God will require of us, before we begin to yearn ardently to possess it. God never grants to any man an unusual spiritual experience unless he has an unusual task awaiting him." In other words God does not give us great power unless we have the courage to use it for good.

When we think of God as we know him in Christ, let us think not so much of the fact that he left the Sermon on the Mount, important as it is, but rather that he left himself for us. On that last day with his disciples he did not say, "Lo, I leave my sermons and my code with you," but *"I leave myself."* "Lo, I am with you alway, even unto the end of the world."

AIDS TO WORSHIP

Hymns: "I Want a Principle Within"
"Saviour, More than Life to Me"
Scripture: "Matt. 28:16-20"

A PRAYER

Eternal God, thou hast been our dwelling place in all generations. Before the mountains were brought forth or ever thou hadst formed the earth and the world, even from everlasting to everlasting, thou art God.

We come before thee this day unworthy of thy love; we come stained by temptations which so easily beset us; we come feeling need of thee—thy power, thy strength, and thy forgiveness. Thou knowest us better than we know ourselves;

72

IDEALS—ALSO POWER TO SEE THEM THROUGH

Thou knowest our needs and art standing ready to help us. Take us this day and lift us upward. Strengthen our steps, enlarge our visions, quicken our hopes, purify our motives. Remind us of the things which do not change, and secure us to life's unfading treasures. In the name and in the spirit of Christ, we pray. AMEN.

15
What about emotion in religion?

ON ONE OCCASION WHEN JESUS WAS ASKED TO NAME
the first and great commandment, he answered by quoting
an ancient Jewish rule: "Thou shalt love the Lord thy
God with all thy heart, and with all thy soul, and with
all thy mind."

It is significant that Jesus first said, "love the Lord thy
God with all thy heart" and followed it by adding "with
all thy mind." He knew the place of emotion in life and
the vital role it plays in our faith. To be sure a religion
without emotion and deep feeling is a waterless sort of
thing without much real life. The heart does make the
world go round. It is the gasoline that runs the motor,
the air that inflates the tires, the dynamo that moves men
to action.

But saying this is not to discount the place of intelligence and reason in religion. We are called upon to love
God not only with our hearts but also with our minds.
Someone has put it clearly in saying that "it is not enough
to say of a person that his heart is in the right place if his
head and hands are in the wrong place." Certainly it is
not enough just to be going places; you must know where
you are going. It is not enough just to have air in your
tires; concern must be given to their use. Men must not

just be impelled to act or move, but also given purpose and direction in that action.

To be sure we must measure a man's love for God not only by his emotional demonstrations, by his intense feelings that surge through his being, but also by the dedication of his mind to God. This we believe.

But having said all this I want to come back to the fact that it is *warm hearts that propel us to action.* It is the emotion that moves us and quickens our will. It is our driving power. It is the fire that makes religion glow.

Certainly there can be no great revival of religion however much intelligence and brains there may be unless it is set on fire, unless there is a surge of feeling that is prompted by God. Religion, to be sure, needs clear thinking but it also must have a vital experience. If it lacks vitality and immediacy it is powerless.

In a real sense, religion without becoming irrational goes beyond reason. We may know the love of God which passes knowledge and understanding. And "to know that love and be filled with God's fullness is to experience the Christian life in a profounder sense than can be set forth in any statement about it," as Charles Holman says. He continues,

So to know God's love is to enter into an experience of rich and satisfying living; it is to find oneself sustained by Powers far beyond human comprehension; it is to achieve a sense of being "at one with the Universe," happily related to one's neighbors and to one's God.

Religion may go beyond reason without being contrary to it in the same way that love goes beyond reason without being contrary to it. "Love, friendship and religion represent different orders of experience from intellectual analysis and the organization of structures of ideas." One is in the area of response and the other control.

We need not be afraid of our emotions in religion. We need not be afraid to express them. We can go to an athletic contest and get all worked up over the game, but when we come to church we are prone to be afraid of deep feeling and emotion. We too often try to steel ourselves against it.

Now to be sure there may be situations where a person with a physical condition has to guard against emotional experiences of intensity of all sorts—at athletic games, in times of sorrow, or at church. But for most of us we need to feel deeply about life and to have our hearts stirred and our minds quickened by God's truth and by his great love and mercy toward us. To come into God's presence with reverence and utter devotion and be lifted upward toward him is to experience that which can mold and deepen life. It is not only an experience enjoyed by men in bygone times, but one that can happen here and now.

Rufus Jones in his book, *A Call to What Is Vital*, tells

of his own experience back in 1886 during a solitary walk in the foothills of the Alps. He says:

> I felt the walls grow thin between the visible and the invisible, and there came a sudden flash of eternity, breaking in on me. I kneeled down then and there in the forest glade, in the sight of the mountains, and dedicated myself in the hush and silence, but in the presence of an invading life, to the work of interpreting the deeper nature of the soul, and direct mystical relation with God, which had already become my major interest.

Out of such an experience a man cannot say only that he knows about God, but also that he knows God. It has to do not only with knowledge but with feeling and emotion.

When the little, blind, deaf, and mute Helen Keller had learned through her patient teacher, Miss Sullivan, to communicate with others, her parents thought that the time had come for her to have religious instruction. She was taken to Phillips Brooks who told her simply about God. And Helen Keller replied, "I have always known that there was such a One, but I did not know His name."

God is a living, revealing, communicating God. And we can feel his presence and have fellowship with him which is to gain entrance into a more abundant life. Thus we are "to love the Lord thy God with all thy heart, and with all thy soul, and with all thy mind."

AIDS TO WORSHIP

Hymns: "O Jesus, I Have Promised"
"Be Strong!"
Scripture: Matt. 21:34-39

A PRAYER

Eternal God, in whom our fathers trusted and in whom we trust, thou hast caused the light of eternal life to shine upon the world. Quicken in us, we beseech thee, the sense of thy gracious Presence here this day.

We come with praise upon our lips and thanksgiving in our hearts. We thank thee for all prophetic spirits who have promised a better day and by their faith helped to usher it in. We thank thee for those men who through the centuries dared to believe in the coming of One who would share men's burdens and free men from sin. And now that he has come, grant us utter faith in him and make us more worthy servants of thine, through Jesus Christ our Lord. AMEN.

78

16
Give it time

WE ARE IMPATIENT PEOPLE. WE WANT WHAT WE
want, when we want it—and that is usually now. We
are not prone to wait. But whether we recognize it or not,
time is a great boon to mankind. It helps heal the wounds
of sorrow; it is needed in all growth; it helps us to forget;
it can clarify our thinking and rightly direct our action.

All of us have had the experience of facing a problem
which seemed insurmountable. No matter how hard we
tried we could not find the right set of answers with which
to solve it. We may have lost sleep over the problem. It
may have brought to us great despair. We saw no way out.
Then we have waited, and the pieces began to fit together.
Light came out of darkness, and the new pattern began
to take shape. New ideas overtook us. Finally, the solution
came.

Byron once wrote:

> Time! the corrector where our judgments err;
> the test of truth, and love; the sole philosopher.

Of course we can make of time an excuse not to decide,
an evasion of duty, or an unwillingness to face or accept
what must be done. But most of us are in danger of rush-
ing in, of demanding now what only time can bring.

79

Faced as we often are with indecision and the frustration that it can bring, we are prone to get it over with and decide hastily when we should wait and give it time.

Surely time is one of the tools of God—to bring healing, to permit growth, to open doors of understanding. Frequently in our scriptures we read these words: "until the time come." For example, we read in Luke 13:35, "Ye shall not see me, until the time come when ye shall say, Blessed is he that cometh in the name of the Lord."

In John 16:12 we have these words of Jesus: "I have yet many things to say unto you, but ye cannot bear them now." Jesus is saying here that time is needed for preparation, for understanding of the truth of God. He is speaking here in his farewell discourse of the frankness with which he has shared the insights he has learned from his Father. But he is telling them that "their spiritual immaturity has unfitted them to learn immediately much that Jesus had in store for them." Revelation to them will be "continued by the Spirit of truth until they can receive it in its fullness."

So, let us be grateful for time which ripens and which brings forth readiness and fullness. When we are faced with a problem, these are not idle words when someone tells us to "sleep on it," for sleep "knits up the ravell'd sleave of care." The morning not only ushers in a new day but heralds new wisdom which only time can bring.

AIDS TO WORSHIP

Hymns: "Love Divine, All Loves Excelling"
"Be Still, My Soul"
Scripture: John 16:1-16

A Prayer

Eternal God, in whom we live and move and have our being, with grateful hearts we lift our prayers unto thee.

We thank thee for this lovely day and for every suggestion of thy presence in our midst. We are grateful for this hour of worship in which we may hear thy voice and feel thee near.

Give us a vision of life at its best. Lift us upward that we may see thy truth and open our hearts that we may receive thy word. Be with all who are in distress this day—the sorrowful, the suffering, the overworked, the unemployed, the sin-sick, and the lost. Bring thy healing love to give release. Take from us dispair and give us hope, through Jesus Christ our Lord. AMEN.

81

17
A time for stock-taking

IN JOHN 6:12 JESUS IS SPEAKING TO HIS DISCIPLES following the feeding of the five thousand with five barley loaves and a couple of fish, and he says: "Gather up the fragments that remain, that nothing be lost," or as another translator has put it, "Gather up the pieces left over, so that nothing may be wasted" (Moffatt).

We marvel at the story of how Jesus was able to take what was at hand and feed a multitude, but let us remember he was concerned not only with the feeding of the multitude but also with what they had left. It expresses his great concern in all life with the remnants which are left, with the wreckage after the storm.

As a matter of fact, the Christian faith has a lot to say about new starts, about building on waste places, about reclaiming what has been lost. Our Lord would have us believe that a man need never despair, that he can always have hope.

How appropriate is this truth for us now and then to turn our minds to new resolutions, new beginnings, new purposes, fresh starts. It is a time for stock-taking, for evaluating, for revamping, for redirecting, remapping.

So is Jesus interested in these lives of ours—not only with what we start life with, but also with what we have left along the way. He came that he might help us gather up the fragments, the leftovers of our lives, and use them for good.

Let us consider today the fragments which circumstances have left us. Few of us get in life the exact circumstances we desire, but most of us are continually being thrown into situations we do not choose and would not have selected. But here they are—what shall we do with them?

Harry Emerson Fosdick has well said that "in man's life, every experience has two aspects, the outer fact and the inner interpretation." It is the combination of these two—outer fact, inner interpretation—which determines the destiny and future of each of us. What happens to us and how we interpret what happens to us—these two parts make the difference.

Of course it goes without saying that the outer facts of life do make a difference. These we cannot ignore. As far as this life is concerned, outer facts do seem to stifle growth, destroy careers, thwart personality, shorten one's span, as well as to enhance one's progress, stimulate one's powers, and bless one's life.

Having said this, however, we now come to the other aspect of life's fragments, inner interpretation. Yes, every experience has two aspects—outer fact, inner interpretation—objective and subjective, the outer play of facts upon us and then our inner interpretation and response to them. And of the two, inner interpretation is the more important. The way we respond to what life offers determines what life means to us. Remember, no one ever finds life worth living; everyone must make life worth living, and that has to do with response.

Of course there are two responses a man may give. He may say: "Look what life has done to me. If it were different, like the opportunity my friend has, what a difference it would make. What can I do in the face of this?"

But those who let the circumstances of life immobilize them, embitter them, never find life's fragments redeemed.

On the other hand there are those who see what life has done and who try to make use of what is left. They gather up the fragments that remain and use them, put a lure in them.

Look at Jesus' life—he was confronted a hundred times with sorrow, bitterness, despair, faithless people, disappointment, cruelty, apparent failure, and, finally, a seemingly untimely death. How did he face such facts? To be sure he did not wish them; in fact he tried to escape them. Hear him there in the garden saying, if there is any other way, God, take me out of this. But when he acknowledged that these facts were ones he could not escape, he then looked at them with a healthy inner interpretation. He saw in them not a cruel, demonlike God, but behind them a Father God who shared his every experience. He saw goodness at the heart of the universe. He saw life working out for the best for those who loved God. And even as he faced the end, in a majestic way, he trusted his all into the hands of his loving Father.

He faced success and did not let it spoil him. He knew how to handle fame. He faced the disappointment of friends and did not lose faith in humanity. He faced the pain of cruel torture and his faith in God wavered not. He was the subject of brutal attack by wicked men and still kept bitterness from his heart and was able to say, "Father, forgive them; for they know not what they do." He faced the lengthening shadows and watched the night come with a trust that caused him to say, "Father, into thy hands I commend my spirit."

And when he tells us to "gather up the fragments that remain, that nothing be lost," we have the assurance that Dwight L. Moody had when he wrote these words in his Bible, "If God is your partner, make your plans big."

God is saying today to you and to me, "Do not give up in despair, for there is still hope. Gather up the fragments that remain, that nothing be lost."

AIDS TO WORSHIP

Hymns: "Thou Hidden Source of Calm Repose"
"Fight the Good Fight"
Scripture: John 6:1-13

A Prayer

Eternal God, we are thankful that thou hast caused the light of life to come forth out of darkness, and that thou hast planted hope within our hearts.

In our satisfaction with mediocre living, we are grateful to turn to thee whose nature is perfection and whose way is unwavering for truth and righteousness. We are thankful that life will not work apart from thee, and that sooner or later we discover it. Be for us our guide when skies are blue as well as our protector in stormy weather. Steady us along life's pilgrimage and strengthen us in facing the tasks committed to our care.

Drive from our lives evil ways and make us over after the likeness of Christ, our Lord, and in his name we pray. AMEN.

86

18
Life needs a saving priority

IN THE SEVENTH VERSE OF THE FOURTH CHAPTER OF Mark we have these words: "Other seed fell among thorns and the thorns grew and choked it, and it yielded no grain" (R.S.V.). Here we have pictured for us by Jesus the strangled life. The roots were still in the soil, but the weeds grew up and choked them, and they yielded no fruit. It is a parable about life today when too often nothing of importance has priority in one's living. Everything is of the same size and importance.

Halford E. Luccock cites for us an example of this in the story of the small boy who, in reading a list of the chief causes of death, was alarmed to discover a new fatal disease. When asked what it was, he answered with one word—"miscellaneous." Millions have died from it. Life has been smothered out by a landslide of miscellaneous things.

A woman, deeply impressed by Arnold Bennett's book *How to Live on Twenty-four Hours a Day* said, "I am going to concentrate." "On what?" asked Bennett. "Oh," she answered, "On lots of things." But the fact is when we concentrate on lots of things we really concentrate on nothing. Life needs a saving priority.

This is what Jesus had in mind when he said, "Seek ye

first the kingdom of God." Concentrate on this first. Certainly if there was danger that life in agricultural, first-century Palestine might be overcrowded, how much more danger there is today in our industrial, gadget-filled age. There are so many more things to choke the world. On every hand we are beckoned; every sense—sight, hearing, touch, smell, taste—is being rushed for attention.

Dr. Luccock puts it this way: "Going through life comes to be like parading before an endless succession of brightly lighted store windows filled with merchandise."

Surely we know now more than ever that the sense men make of life is determined by what claims their deepest attention. The question is: "What are the priorities of life?" For what do we reserve seats in our souls? What occupies those seats determines not only what we find in life here but also our destiny.

George Buttrick says that the novelist Alexander Black was fond of asking, "If you were to receive a million dollars tomorrow, what would you do with it?" It was his way of finding out what came first in a person's life. What does come first? To be sure a man must think about food and clothing, but he should not think about them first.

Psychologists distinguish for us what is marginal and what is focal in our attention. When we are intent upon a book, we may be marginally aware of the temperature of the room and the ticking of the clock, but as the book grows in interest these marginal impressions are dimmed.

Our lives are crowded today. We fill them with activity—going places and doing things. We are impatient even to miss a green light. Consequently, we are in danger of crowding out the really important things of life. Jesus knew this when he said, "Seek ye first the kingdom of God, and his righteousness." He knew that if the things of the spirit became marginal, crowded out, then life would become a merry-go-round of meaningless activity.

S. Parkes Cadman once said to a group of church women:

It is not easy to keep close to the Cross in an age when luxuries are every woman's right, and when she may have, by pressing an electric button, comforts and conveniences not known in the age of Queen Victoria.

The tremendous increase in scientific invention has given women opportunities to see and do more in a day than their grandmothers did in ten years, but there has not been a corresponding spiritual growth. We need today a better and deeper religious life. We need to get young people to love Christ.

The greatest peril of the present generation is the tendency to give the center of the stage to things which do not matter.

Vida Scudder puts it like this: "Life's drama is smothered in details; 'tis largely composed of irrelevancies." That is, life is crowded with the things that do not really matter.

"Seek ye first the kingdom of God, and his righteousness; and all these things shall be added unto you."

AIDS TO WORSHIP

Hymns: "Jesus, Keep Me Near the Cross"
            "Walk in the Light"
Scripture: Matt. 6:19-34

A PRAYER

O God, our lives are as open books to thy understanding. Forgive us, we pray, for our misdeeds. We are not asking that thou wouldst free us from the pains of our sins nor the wages that they surely bring, but that thou wouldst give us another chance and the strength to withstand temptations encompassing our daily lives. Give us the courage to confess our sins and the willingness to make amends for the wrong we have done.

Grant that our experiences may make us know that in our own strength we cannot overcome the temptations of life, but only as we live daily within thy presence, and draw goodness from thee who art the source of all goodness—only so can we live victoriously. In Christ's name we pray. AMEN.

19

Just around the corner

(New Year's Day)

WE HAVE NOW MOVED INTO A NEW YEAR. RESOLUTIONS have been made and many of them already broken. But the year ahead is still fresh in the early days of its beginning. We are still writing the old year on our dated letters and checks.

Civic groups are asking the wisest in the world of business to look into the crystal ball and forecast what we are to expect in the year ahead. Recently, a man attended one such meeting and heard a banker, a steel executive, a utility head, and a wholesale business president predict for them what now seems likely for the months ahead. True, there are signs of the time which give grounds for prediction, but the fact remains that most of the new year is an unknown frontier stretching out before us. We do not know what is just around the corner.

Leslie Weatherhead tells of a meeting he had with Hugh Redwood, the journalist, who told him how on one occasion he was living under severe strain and anxiety, not knowing which way to turn concerning a decision that

91

had to be made. He went to a friend's house just prior to a speaking engagement, and his friend said to him, "You look tired. Would you like to escape all this chatter and rest in a room upstairs?" When he went to the room upstairs, he found to his delight a fireplace bright with burning logs and an easy chair drawn up near the fire. By the chair on the table was an open Bible, opened at the fifty-ninth psalm, and in the margin opposite verse ten were pencil marks giving an interpretation of the verse. Reading that verse and its interpretation kindled his imagination and sent him on his way with new assurance.

The verse reads, "The God of my mercy shall prevent me," and the word "prevent" means "go before." But the penciled interpretation ran like this: "My God in his lovingkindness shall meet me at every corner." Those were just the words he needed. They helped him make his decision, and he turned his corner with assurance. But these words speak not only to the need of a journalist who has spent a long and useful career, but to us all as we face the unexpected turns of this year.

Let us make this truth our very own: "My God in his lovingkindness shall meet me at every corner." We do not know what the year holds, what is just around the corner; but we can be assured that God will be there waiting for us as we come to those corners. Life is made up of unexpected experiences which make special demands upon us, and what we make of it will depend upon whether we turn our corners with fear or with faith, with cowardice or with courage, with anxiety or with serenity. How then are we to meet our corners in this new year?

First, let us keep our eyes focused not so much on ourselves as on God and his will. Let us not ask always what it is we want, but what God wants. Let us be sure we are seeking to do his will, knowing that his will and his plans for our lives are best for us. We need to get out of ourselves and to get into the bigness and majesty of God. In the fret and turmoil of these times we need to fasten our minds and thoughts upon the greatness and majesty of God.

Go out some dark night and look up at the stars. If you remember the words of the Psalmist, "The heavens declare the glory of God; and the firmament sheweth his handywork," then the stars seem to say to you, "Don't fret, you are very small, but remember your God will meet you at the corner. He is great enough to take care of you." Look again and hear them say, "Don't fret! What's troubling you is not nearly as big as it seems."

Jesus made it a practice of his life to look away from himself to God. Even when he felt alone and forsaken, he called God his "Father."

When we focus our minds upon God, faith helps us to see that this is God's world and that he is just and that his divine leadership can be trusted. When things go wrong, we can look at God and know that we can still

93

trust in his love and mercy and that "all things work to-gether for good to them that love God." The man of faith knows that God is going to have the last word in our world, and he rests his future in his hands.

Let us then live, not with the fevered rush that comes from anxiety and dread, but with assurance—the assurance that we are in the care and keeping of a loving Father who meets us at every corner and whose strength is sufficient for our every need. With Paul let us pray, "I can do all things through Christ which strengeneth me."

A man faced a corner that was filled with fear and fore-boding. He needed to have a serious operation, and after-wards he said, "I was not afraid; I found the spiritual help needed to see me through." God met him at this unex-pected corner.

Leslie Weatherhead reminds us that Christ looked away to God and is saying to us something like this:

Your Father knows. He understands and cares. He has got your situation in hand. He will tell you what to do. He is the Lord of history, the Master of everything we call accident, the Weaver of all our sins and failures and sorrows into His inde-structible plans, and He is the Victor over death.

So we, too, can say with confidence, "My God in His lovingkindness shall meet me at every corner." At every corner of anxiety, sorrow, pain, loss—and even in death, the last corner—we can say "though I walk through the valley of the shadow of death, I will fear no evil: for thou art with me."

AIDS TO WORSHIP

Hymns: "This Is My Father's World"
"In the Hour of Trial"

Scripture: Ps. 27

A PRAYER

Eternal God, thou who hast made us and who dost care for us, we thank thee for this thy world—our dwelling place. Thou hast richly furnished it for our use.

We are grateful for new life which greets us every day, for the stirring of nature from winter's sleep, for the soil and sunshine, for floating clouds and the rain, for the beauty of thy earth.

We thank thee, not only for life's joys and pleasures, but for thy presence and care in life's sorrows and suffering. We cannot explain why we are allowed to suffer, but we know that thou art good and that thou dost will for us the best. We are assured that underneath our lives art thy everlasting arms. Be especially near this day to all who lie on beds of pain. Sustain and strengthen them, we pray. Give to those who watch beside them—often in helpless waiting—thy assurance.

Grant that all of us may live so close to thee that when illness comes, we may be victorious sufferers, through Jesus Christ our Lord. AMEN.

95

20
Learn to live together

(Brotherhood Sunday)

DURING THE LAST HUNDRED YEARS MANKIND HAS MADE amazing scientific advancement. We have witnessed far-fetched dreams come true. Pushing buttons and turning switches of machines which now do the work that once our hands had to do makes us wonder how men survived a hundred years ago. We have come to the place where no prediction, however fantastic, surprises us.

But the tragedy of our times is that we remain in the pre-scientific age as far as our attitudes and relations—group with group, nation with nation, and race with race—are concerned. We come to this modern scene in a mood of fear and despair, for we now see that much of our so-called progress was pseudo progress. Yes, man has shortened space and to some degree lengthened time with his laborsaving devices; yet, with all his progress man is becoming the victim of that which he has made. Winston Churchill prophetically said in 1924:

Mankind has never been in this position before. Without having improved appreciably in virtue or enjoying wiser guidance, it has got into its hands for the first time the tools by which it can unfailingly accomplish its own extermination.

96

Now we are coming to see that men must learn to live together as brothers or else die together as enemies. We here in America are composed of many population groups. There are people here from about fifty nations who call this land home. We are divided into many religious groups —in fact, over two hundred. Some of us were foreign-born; others of us, American-born. We are white men, American Indians, Negroes, Americans from the Philippines, Mexico, China, and Japan. We live in the cities and on the farm. We belong to the ranks of management and labor or of the professions. And yet, from such diversity, we all claim to be Americans and are committed to a way of life that extends to everyone the rights we want to keep for ourselves. This way can be maintained if we protect and nurture that will to co-operate and if we see to it that it outstrips the temptations to divide and quarrel. It is not only good religion to co-operate, but it is also common sense.

Our land can become a beacon of hope to a troubled humanity by demonstrating that people of every nation, culture, and religious persuasion can live side by side as peaceful neighbors when they all really try. The late Franklin D. Roosevelt said, "The perpetuation of democracy depends upon the practice of the brotherhood of men."

Roman Catholic, Jewish, and Protestant groups believe together that what the world needs today is more goodness. The fact is that there is not enough goodness to go around. And we further agree that if there is to be more goodness, it must come from the source of all goodness—God. In the final analysis brotherhood is dependent upon a conception of God which makes us all related. It finds its roots nourished and sustained in the faith which believes in the Fatherhood of God. Let us each in his own way seek to worship him who is the source of all goodness and head of the family of all men, and to remember those immortal words inscribed on the Statue of Liberty:

> Give me your tired, your poor,
> Your huddled masses yearning to breathe free
> The wretched refuse of your teeming shore.
> Send those, the homeless, tempest-tost to me,
> I lift my lamp beside the golden door!

AIDS TO WORSHIP

Hymns: "Dear Lord and Father of Mankind"
"Once to Every Man and Nation"
Scripture: Acts 17:22-28

A PRAYER

O God, who hast made of one blood all nations of men; help us to know that thou art the Father of us all and that we are brothers one to another. We thank thee that no barrier of race or clan may keep men from thee. We are all members of thy great family and need to learn from thee how to live as brothers. Thou would have us to live together in con-

cord and peace. Help us who have been so favored to learn
how to share, how to appreciate, those who through chance
are denied so much in life.

Forbid that we should harbor false pride of race or nation-
ality, but breathe into our beings a deep humility. Give us
mature minds that will help us understand the crisis of men
today. Give us clear visions that we may judge men by what
they are and not by what group they are in.

Take us, lift us, inspire us, strengthen us, through Jesus
Christ our Lord. AMEN.

99

21

The Cross confronts the
modern world

(Lent)

HOLY WEEK IS THE MOST SIGNIFICANT WEEK IN ALL history when, on Palm Sunday, Jesus Christ rode triumphantly into Jerusalem. The masses of people were cheering, declaring him king. What a week lay before him! What events were packed into that week!

Moving into the week the institution of the Lord's Supper took its first form as Jesus gathered his disciples in that upper room. What a moving scene this was!—a little band of men with all their human frailties assembled around this one perfect man who was foretelling his own doom.

Reluctantly they believed him; and even so, with little understanding. There was Peter who denied him, Judas who betrayed him, and even doubting Thomas—all partook of this first supper on Thursday evening.

Following the betrayal and arrest, came the mock trial with a padded jury of ecclesiastics whose position Jesus threatened. Then looming up in all of its tragedy and yet in all of its dazzling brilliance was the Cross, forever to be the symbol of the Christian faith.

Then came Easter Day—the Resurrection!

What events crowded into that one week! There has been no other like it in human history. What occurred then has changed the course of mankind.

So, let us lift before our mind's eye one event of the week which has towered over "the wrecks of time." Let us again take a look at the Cross as it confronts the modern world.

In the first place, the Cross confronts the modern world with the depths of sin. We see in it life at its worst confronting life at its best. Here is sin in all its stark reality; for the fact of the Cross is the result of the fact of sin. Nothing but evil in the hearts of men could do this to a man who had done no harm.

Jesus was one who went about doing good—healing the blind, causing the lame to walk, bringing new hope to the fallen, restoring self-respect in the outcast, pointing men to the only way life will work. He was kind, tender, courageous, loving.

He asked no favors in return for the good he did except that men should give their lives to God. But cruel and evil men feared the light he brought lest it reveal the darkness of their lives. His goodness threatened their meanness, so they crucified him.

And wherever we find sin today, we can find a cross and can be reminded of that cross on Calvary hill which

crucified God's son. When we are tempted to take it
lightly and try to ignore it by calling it such names as
ignorance, unfulfilled good, human error or mistake, let us
turn our eyes to that cross outside Jerusalem and know
that sin always does that to life.

Yet, in spite of life's tragedy today many of us take
lightly the seriousness of sin. Reinhold Niebuhr has said
that "modern man has an essentially easy conscience."
Too often we have followed Plato's conception of sin as
ignorance, echoing the words of Socrates that no man
knowingly does wrong. But Niebuhr says that sin is certainly not ignorance but is basically pride and self-righteousness. We have too often groomed it, powdered and painted
it, so as to make it look respectable; but whether it be
living on a fashionable boulevard in a brick mansion or
in a wooden shack by the side of a railroad track, it is still
sin.

Now let us think not merely in general terms but in
more specific terms. All of us stand in need of repentance.
All of us have a measure of pride and self-righteousness,
the like of which crucified our Lord. You remember the
words of the Negro spiritual which asks the question:
"Were you there when they crucified my Lord?" In a
deep sense we were all there, for we harbor within ourselves today those same sinful qualities which lead to
the Cross.

Again, the Cross confronts us not only with the depths

102

of sin, but also with the power of sacrificial love. In this sacrificial act we find life's most powerful force. The power of the Cross has lifted the world. Jesus said: "And I, if I be lifted up . . . will draw all men unto me."

Sacrificial love melts hard hearts. It captures seasoned criminals. It causes a Judas, realizing what he has done, to fling himself upon a jagged rock. It turns enemies into friends. It is a love that goes beyond what is expected.

We cannot get away from it. Several years ago a soldier wounded in the South Pacific was sent home to be hospitalized. He was still trying to find the name of the corporal who had saved his life. In a hopeless situation this corporal had crawled and carried him to safety and then had disappeared. Who was he? The soldier wants to know and will always want to know. We cannot get away from such a sacrificial act.

God knew that the only way to capture the hearts of men was through the sacrificial goodness of his son, and his love was so great that he was willing to do it. Mankind may evade and sidestep such affection for a time, but it can never get away from it. "And I, if I be lifted up . . . will draw all men unto me."

AIDS TO WORSHIP

Hymns: "Beneath the Cross of Jesus"
"When I Survey the Wondrous Cross"
Scripture: Mark 15:16-41

A PRAYER

O thou eternal God, who hast made thyself known supremely in the coming of Jesus Christ our Lord, we rejoice that once again we may turn our eyes back to that event which has altered the course of history. We marvel at his birth, his life, his teaching; but especially are we grateful for his presence here among us. We thank thee that thou didst send him as a Saviour of mankind, a Redeemer who lifts us from our sins, and a Companion who travels with us along life's way.

During these days leading toward Easter, we remember his passion and sacrifice for sinful humanity; we remember his death and resurrection which have changed the course of history, and which offer eternal life to all who believe on his name.

Grant, our Father, that we may become more worthy of such love; and during these days may we discipline ourselves to become fit channels of thy love. Take us as we are and make us over through Christ our Lord. AMEN.

22
The assurance of Easter

IN THE TWENTY-EIGHTH CHAPTER OF MATTHEW WE have recorded how Mary Magdalene and the other Mary went in the early dawn of that first Easter morn to see the tomb. But an angel spoke to them and said, "Do not be afraid; for I know that you seek Jesus who was crucified. He is not here; for he has risen, as he said. Come, see the place where he lay." (R.S.V.)

Thus on Easter we come back again and again to hear these words spoken and to find in them that which gives us hope. We come, not merely because we want to see and be seen, but because deep down we seek for renewed hope about life and life eternal.

Certainly we feel that unless there is more to life than we sometimes suspect there is, then indeed it is not worth living. Unless the way to which Jesus pointed is true, there is little hope for any of us. Time and time again we come to an impasse which confronts us with the fact that we cannot carry on in our own strength. The strains of daily living, the misunderstandings in our homes, the burdens that grief places upon us, the temptations that easily beset us—these weigh heavily upon us and break our backs unless we turn to "everlasting arms" which can uphold us.

Thus, these three words—"He has risen"—become the dominant note for Easter and indeed the watershed of history. More than this, they become for us our greatest *hope*. Let us look then today at the assurance which Easter brings.

In the first place, here is the assurance of the fact of Easter—the fact of the Resurrection. At first the disciples were stunned by the news and the evidence of the Resurrection. It was incredible as good news; but it became credible good news. It was too good to be true. Doubting Thomas wanted to be shown; then he believed. But the fact of the Resurrection does not rest primarily on the gospel accounts of it. Far more convincing "has been the historic fact of the Christian Church with its unceasing testimony to an indwelling Lord."

A man looking for the first time at Grand Canyon said, after a period of silent awe, "Gee! Something must have happened here!" Halford E. Luccock has commented saying, "It was rather obvious. It was evident that that deep gash in the earth was not made by an Indian drawing a stick along the ground." So we can look at the right-about-face of the disciples, the creation of the church, and say, "Something must have happened here." The only adequate "something" is the resurrection of Jesus. It is a fact. It is a fact that quickened the Christian church and sustained it through the years. The impact of Christ's resurrection hurled missionaries twenty-five thousand miles

106

around the globe and has shaken the earth for nineteen centuries.

So, when we look back on that first Easter and the events which followed, the most convincing evidence of the Resurrection is the new power in life and death which the world saw in changed men. There was something which transformed Simon into the rocklike Peter and which changed the bigoted young Pharisee, Saul of Tarsus, into the Christlike Paul. "It was not," as someone has said, "the memory of a Galilean Carpenter, but the resurrection and the Living Christ which made Jesus the chief regenerative power in the world's history."

Thus, we have the assurance of the fact of the Resurrection. "Lo, I am with you alway, even unto the end of the world."

In the second place, here is the assurance of the promise of Easter. When Jesus said, "Because I live, ye shall live also," and when he triumphed over the grave that first Easter, then it was that man gained his greatest assurance of life after death.

Men have always been interested in the question: "If a man die, shall he live again?" There is that within us which longs, if not for ourselves, for the continuance of life of those we love and admire. We see in the pyramids of Egypt, as well as in the burial mounds of American Indians—from such widely different civilizations—longings for an Eternal tomorrow. A child once asked, "What is behind the sunset?" This is the final question, the answer to which all men seek.

John Rathbone Oliver tells of a young physician friend of his who met an untimely death. He had been married to a young girl, and they were a devoted couple, deeply in love. Then tragedy struck when, through a chance infection from an autopsy, the young physician died. They had been married only a year.

Dr. Oliver confesses with shame that he did not go to the funeral. He had written so much about overcoming fear, but yet he was afraid to look at the young woman. He avoided her on every hand. He did not write her, although they were old friends. Finally one morning, quite by accident, he saw her outside the hospital. She wore no black; there was nothing about her to suggest depressive hopelessness. He says, "Her face was alight with something more than mere happiness."

He mumbled some lame excuse about not having seen her sooner. She smiled and said, "Ah, Doctor, you don't understand. I miss Dick. Of course I miss him. But I haven't room in my heart for anything but thankfulness and gratitude to God. I had a year of Dick's love—a whole year of perfect happiness. No other woman has had as much as I. If I live to be eighty, I shall not have had time to thank God enough. And when I do stop living—well, Dick and I will begin living together again."

The Easter promise had meaning for her.

As Christians we come again to this blessed Easter morning to have our faith strengthened and our hope quickened. We watch the darkness and despair those early disciples faced after Good Friday. We see how for them the light had gone out. Today, however, we see once again that on the following Sunday morning they could cry with joy, "The Lord is risen!" Since that time this has been the crowning glory of the Christian faith with all its varied meanings. Now we have something to hold on to. Now death holds no hopeless fear; for death was robbed of its sting, the grave of its victory. Now we hear those words, "Because I live, ye shall live also," and they become for us another sunrise.

AIDS TO WORSHIP

Hymns: "Christ the Lord Is Risen Today"
          "Crown Him with Many Crowns"
Scripture: Matt. 28:1-8

A Prayer

Eternal God, thou who makest the stars and turnest the shadow of death into the morning, we thank thee for the resurrection of the springtime, for the everlasting hopes that rise within the human heart, and for the gospel which has brought life and immortality to light.

Prepare our minds and hearts for this blessed season; make us conscious of our sins and shortcomings. As we think of those forces which lead to the crucifixion of our Lord, help us to see in ourselves the sins which lead to his death. Recall to our minds the sacrifices which were his that we may know better the height and depth of thy love.

Make us rejoice that the darkness could not hold him but that he is alive forevermore, through Jesus Christ our Lord. AMEN.

23
God bless our homes
(Mother's Day)

WHEN WE THINK OF MOTHER'S DAY AND ALL THAT IT signifies, a lump comes into our throats. We think of one who believes in us, who stands by us when the going is good and when it is rough, who binds up our wounds and comforts us in our sorrows. We think of one who forgets herself to answer our every need, who feels that no sacrifice is too great for the good of her child.

It is fitting that one day out of the year be set aside to do her honor and to see with fresh eyes her task and its significance for today's world. There are those who say, "Let's not get sentimental about this day. Let's keep it from becoming mushy and superficial."

But the danger in this practical, cash-and-carry world is not that we might overindulge in sentiment, but that we might miss the tender and noble meaning of motherhood, that we might pass over the rightful place of the home in our lives.

Some time ago a minister was in a home which had an old-fashioned sampler hanging on the wall with its cross-stitches reading: "Home Sweet Home." The good woman of that house told him that the sampler came from her mother's home and was well over one hundred years old.

And we have seen other samplers reading "God Bless Our Home."

We need to go back to the days of yesterday and weave into the fabric of our modern life some of the virtues of yesterday's home. There is no better description of the best in yesterday's home than given by Grace Noll Crowell in her matchless poem:

So Long as There Are Homes

So long as there are homes to which men turn
 At the close of day,
So long as there are homes where children are,
 Where women stay,
If love and loyalty and faith be found
 Across these sills,
A stricken nation can recover from
 Its gravest ills.

So long as there are homes where fires burn
 And there is bread,
So long as there are homes where lamps are lit
 And prayers are said;
Although a people falters through the dark
 And nations grope,
With God himself back of these little homes
 We still can hope.[2]

Let's see from this poem some of the things we need to keep today.

[2] From *Light of the Years* by Grace Noll Crowell. Copyright 1936 by Harper & Brothers. Used by permission.

"So long as there are homes . . . *Where women stay.*"
This doesn't mean that just because there is a woman in the home, that because someone is there to cook the meals and wash dirty faces, that it will be a blessed home. We know better than that. We know that there are homes in our land today which are not conducive to fruitful living, because there is a woman in the home.

And yet, as Grace Noll Crowell so well says:

> If love and loyalty and faith be found
> Across these sills,
> A stricken nation can recover from
> Its gravest ills.

She is saying that where women who have love and loyalty and faith stay, they indeed bless our homes. These are the ones to whom honor is due today. These are the ones who have preserved the virtues of yesterday's homes for today.

"So long as there are homes where lamps are lit and *prayers are said.*"

Here our poet is thinking of religion in the home—a beyond loyalty that becomes a tie that binds, that cements us together. How our little families need a reference beyond themselves to which they may give themselves!

Who of us here today has not felt the strains of modern living making their inroads into the home? The president

113

of a Midwestern college once said to a friend: "You know many nights I come home worn and tired by the affairs of the college and find myself irritable with those I love."

To be sure we are caught in the middle of a noisy, nervous world. We tend to be weakened and worried by the pressures of modern living. What we need is frequent attachment to the things which do not change. We need to remind ourselves of those assurances found in the twenty-third psalm.

If you and I in our homes would try repeating this psalm every morning before we leave for our daily tasks, quietness would come to our nerves. If we would repeat it during the day and at night, deeper peace would take hold of our lives in our homes, and we would be kinder to those we love.

Herbert Gray of England is right when he says, "Marriages fail because people fail, and people fail because they live without God."

"So long as there are homes where lamps are lit and prayers are said."

And if prayers are to be said, to the mother goes the greatest responsibility. For it is at a mother's knee a child first learns "Now I lay me down to sleep." From a mother's lips he first repeats his good-night prayers.

And then, the poet says, "With God himself back of these little homes we still can hope!"

114

Nothing can separate us when he is behind our homes.

Let us recall again the simple sampler with the meaningful words found so frequently in the homes of yesterday, "*God Bless Our Home.*" And if we weave the sentiment of these words into the fabric of American home life we need not fear the future.

AIDS TO WORSHIP

Hymns: "Happy the Home When God Is There"
"O Love Divine and Golden"

Scripture: I Cor. 13 4 -6

A PRAYER

Eternal God, we are grateful that thou didst see fit to place us in homes where love is and parents are. Especially we offer to thee our gratitude for the sweet ministries of motherhood in human life and for the love of our own mothers. As children help us to be worthy of her love and faithful to her trust in us. Forbid that we should forget her many deeds of kindness, her tireless love, her voiceless prayers, and her willing sacrifices. Help us so to live that our lives may reflect honor upon her name.

And to all mothers, give them the true sense of their mission and place in life. Help them to be noble and true, reflecting thy mercy and goodness to us. In Christ's name we pray. AMEN.

24
How God measures a man

(Father's Day)

SUNDAY IS FATHER'S DAY! IT IS SIGNIFICANT THAT IT was a woman who started this now-traditional observance. Her name is Mrs. John Bruce Dodd of Spokane, Washington. Her father, William Smart, was a father and "mother" to the family of six. The mother died early and Mrs. Dodd interested her state's governor in a state-wide tribute to fathers. It was first held in 1910, while the first Mother's Day celebration was held in 1912.

Some years ago there were some statistics compiled from the United States census. They indicated that the average father is forty-four years old, and the chances are nine to one that he lives with his wife and one to two children. The chances are three to two that he lives in a town of 25,000 people or more, and that he is a native-born son of parents who were born here.

Two-and-a-half million American fathers have an infant son or daughter, in any given year, and that includes about 25,000 sets of twins, 274 of triplets, and two of quadruplets. One American father, during this particular year the census was taken, had twenty-seven children.

So today, we salute you who are fathers! We honor the

fathers of our land and pray that they will live up to the opportunities and responsibilities which are theirs.

Several years ago a poll was taken of fifteen hundred children around thirteen years old in Massachusetts schools and they were asked what person they wanted to be like ten years from that date. It is a sobering consideration to know that only 10 per cent said they wanted to be like dad!

So, it is well for us today to consider just what are some of God's measurements of a man.

In the first psalm we have pictured for us the contrasting view of two ways a man can live. There is the righteous way and the unrighteous way. The career of the righteous man is first considered negatively. "Blessed is the man that walketh not in the counsel of the ungodly, nor standeth in the way of sinners, nor sitteth in the seat of the scornful." He has nothing to do with evil men, thereby escaping their influence. The man who associates with evil men may, at first, merely walk with them, but soon he stands where sinners congregate, and at last he sits with them as one of their scoffing company.

But the righteous man delights in the law of the Lord. The Psalmist compares him to "a tree planted by the rivers of water, that bringeth forth his fruit in his season; his leaf also shall not wither; and whatsoever he doeth shall prosper." He is like a tree on the bank of a stream which has a constant source of refreshment. This makes him regular in his good fruitage.

What, then, is the measure of a man from God's point of view? God judges man, not by his outward acts alone, but by his inward motives and attitudes. He judges men by their genuine worth, not by their surface appearance. He judges men by the quality of their lives.

In the twenty-third chapter of Matthew, Jesus says, "Woe to you, scribes and Pharisees, hypocrites! For you cleanse the outside of the cup and of the plate, but inside they are full of extortion and rapacity. You blind Pharisee! First cleanse the inside of the cup and of the plate, that the outside also may be clean."

"Woe to you, scribes and Pharisees, hypocrites! for you are like whitewashed tombs, which outwardly appear beautiful, within they are full of dead men's bones and all uncleanness." (R.S.V.)

It is what is inside that makes the difference with God.

Frederick H. Pough of the American Museum of Natural History tells of a method used by dishonest jewel dealers to change and improve the color of cheap stones by X-ray treatment and thus increase their value. When treated with X-ray white topax changes to brown-purple, pinkish sapphires turn to brilliant amber. These changes remain so long as the stones are kept in the dark and at room temperature. But when exposed to heat and light, they revert to their original color. But there are some stones, like emeralds and opals, which show no change under X-ray treatment and thus defy fraud.

Charles M. Crowe, in commenting on this, says that men are like precious stones. At times they absorb the coloration from exposure to a Christian environment which allows them to pass for more than they are really worth. Sometimes they take on a coating of culture and respectability for the sake of a short-term objective. They change colors to meet changing circumstances.

And so long as conditions are favorable they remain undetected. But when they are tested by some strong temptation, they show their true colors. When faced with a bitter experience or exposed to the white light of God's truth, they often revert to type.

God does not, however, measure a man by some surface appearance, but by the way he stands up to favorable and unfavorable circumstances. The true measure of a man is determined by what is in his soul rather than by his capacity to change color with his environment. God judges him by whether he rings true when the testing time comes.

It may be a testing time of misfortune, of temptation, of sickness, of tragedy, of success. The true test comes when a man is off guard more than when he is on guard. What about the motive, the purpose, the heart, the soul? These are God's instruments of measurement.

God honors men whose lives are just and righteous. His

standard of measurement is not how smart we are or how much money we have, but rather what we are. How honest, how just, how loving, truthful, and pure we are—this is his measurement of a man. And "he shall be like a tree planted by the rivers of water."

AIDS TO WORSHIP

Hymns: "Are Ye Able?"
        "Once to Every Man and Nation"
Scripture: Ps. 1

A PRAYER

Eternal God, in whose world we live and from whom we gain strength for our days, we lift our hearts to thee this day in praise and adoration. We thank thee for the heritage that is ours, for the dreams and ideals which have been handed down to us, for this our native land and our priceless treasures of freedom.

Be especially near today to all fathers upon whose shoulders rest heavy cares. Grant them strength to fulfill their tasks. Give them a clear vision of the place they hold. Help them to be true to the meaning of fatherhood as given by Christ our Lord. Guide them that they may become worthy examples for younger feet to follow. Strengthen them in the face of temptation and confirm them in the faith.

Help us all to be true to the highest we know, to follow the truth as we see it, and to give ourselves into thy care and keeping, through Jesus Christ our Lord. AMEN.

120

25
Finding meaning in your job
(*Labor Sunday*)

THE TRAGEDY OF THESE TIMES IS THAT SO MANY
millions of people have lost the sense of dignity of the
day's work. They see no real meaning in their job. It is
just something that has to be done to keep soul and body
together. Apart from the weekly pay envelope or the
monthly check there is no real meaning in it.

For some the idea of work is that of one hitchhiker
who said to the other, "That's right, just sit there and
let me work my finger to the bone."

But surely if we are going to find joy in life and satisfaction in our living, we must see meaning and purpose
in our jobs. How can we do this? Here are some helpful
suggestions others have found to be true:

First, let us realize that every job has its own set of
difficulties and its own set of satisfactions.

Sometimes the job that we have seems to be made up
only of the unpleasant. The detail and routine almost get
us down. Then we think of someone else's job and we see
in it only pleasantness. But don't forget that every job
is made up of both aspects.

Second, any job which is worth while can have more
meaning if you give to it interest and imagination.

121

Learn all you can about your job. Read everything you can find that will make you better informed about it. Many times we will discover that there is far more to what we are doing then we realized.

This leads us to our main consideration, namely, if our work is to have more meaning let us try to see how our little jobs are part of a larger setting.

When we see what we are doing as part of a great scheme of things, we become conscious that we are making a contribution to the common work of the world. Of course we must recognize that some work seems to be more worth while than others, and that some is not worth while at all. There are jobs into which good men are ashamed to enter and from which others leave because they are not worth while.

Elton Trueblood tells of a man employed by a well-known distillery who sought a complete change. Why did he change? Here is his story: "Well, it's hard to express, but perhaps it is that, at the end of the day, I want to feel that I've pulled my weight." He knew that life is short, and he didn't want to come to the end of it feeling ashamed, feeling forced to admit that he had never done anything except help to make a little whiskey.

All of us want to feel that what we are doing is worthwhile, that our efforts are being directed toward some achievement, no matter how modest. Life is unbearable unless it has real meaning, and the way for it to have meaning is to be engaged in work which we know is contributing to some larger whole.

Finally, each job can be interpreted in human terms, as a venture in helping people, as part of God's plan for his world.

Hiram Goff, the cobbler, was one who saw real meaning in his job in its relationship to the whole scheme of things. Listen to his story.

I am a shoemaker by the grace of God. Just look at that (and he took up the battered shoe of a child). That shoe belongs to a little fellow of six. If he should catch cold some muddy day and get pneumonia his father might lose his child. Now then, I propose to mend those shoes as though my salvation depended on it. God is saying to me, "Hiram, I have sot you to makin' shoes, and I want you to make 'em good; don't put no paper in the soles for the sake of a little profit; and see that the uppers is well tanned.' Every time I pull a thread I want to say to myself, "There! that stitch will hold! I've put my religion into it!"

To be sure God calls his servants into the Christian ministry, but likewise he calls them into every area of life that is contributing to the welfare of mankind. It is just as important for one boy to decide to be a Christian businessman as it is for another boy to decide to be a Christian minister.

Part of our trouble, as Elton Trueblood has pointed out, is that we have left the religious job to those who

123

are supposed to be professionally religious. But the task is too large for any one group but need all dedicated to it.

There are now encouraging signs of the enlargement of the idea of vocation. Recently a group of businessmen met with a ministerial association for lunch. They represented the Gideon Society, made up of businessmen who are devoted to the task of distributing Bibles in hotels, schools, jails, hospitals, and other places where needed. They are doing a wonderful job. Trueblood points out how in Washington there is a little group of legislators who now meet regularly for prayer, because they look upon their work of lawmaking as a holy calling.

If we could but see in our work its larger purpose, then our jobs would take on new meaning. The work of a bricklayer is magnified if it helps to erect buildings in which men may work, live, and worship. Sweeping a hotel room can be important if it helps to re-create the lives of those who occupy that room so that they may devote themselves to some noble goal. A Pullman porter makes a real contribution in serving people who are able to serve others. Motherhood is the most satisfying vocation of all, for the mother extends her life into the lives of her children, and thus her kind deeds live on.

We want to do work that lasts. The Psalmist speaks of this desire when he prays this prayer which may become our own: "Establish thou the work of our hands, [O Lord]."

124

AIDS TO WORSHIP

Hymns: "O Lord and Father of Mankind"
"O Master, Let Me Walk with Thee"
Scripture: Ps. 90

A PRAYER

O God, whose Son Jesus was once carpenter at Nazareth, we pray thee for the workers of the world. Thankfully we come unto thee who has made all worthy labor honorable, who through thy Son showed us that work with our hands is dignified. May we see in the tasks at hand our share in thy Kingdom's building. Grant that our work be spiritualized, that its usefulness be given purpose, and that its drudgery give way to the fuller meaning of its ministry.

Whatever we do, O God, whether it be behind a loom, in a shop, behind a desk, over a stove, across a counter, in a field—may it all be turned to thee for sanction and direction. Send us out today with new faith and hope to be used in the building of thy great Kingdom on earth, through Jesus Christ our Lord. AMEN.

125

26
Keeping our desires high
(World Peace Sunday)

WE CANNOT IGNORE THE KIND OF WORLD IN WHICH WE
as Christians live anymore than we can ignore the air we
breathe. The late Archbishop of Canterbury, William
Temple, says in his book, *The Church Looks Forward*,

The Christian tradition is challenged from without more
powerfully than in any period since the end of the Dark
Ages, and is in danger of being undermined by a secular
humanism which hopes to retain Christian values without
Christian faith.

Elton Trueblood in his *Predicament of Modern Man*
characterizes, in his now-famous words, our age as being
a "cut-flower civilization." And beautiful as cut flowers
may be, they will eventually die because they are severed
from their sustaining roots. In many areas of life we are
trying to maintain the dignity of the individual apart from
the deep faith that every man is made in the image of God
and is important in his sight.

We are now coming to see that ethical convictions
cannot long prevail apart from religious roots. No longer
is it popular to debate the relationship between religion
and morals on college campuses, as it was decades ago.

Many are coming to see with clearer insight that religious roots cannot be nourished apart from the organized church or something like it.

We are coming also to see that in the final analysis, more important than man's ability and his efficiency—important as both of these are—are his goodness, his motive, his purpose in life. We now see the necessity of learning to care for the right sort of things. We see the danger of a highly skilled civilization with a low-leveled motive.

This is what Thomas Huxley had in mind when in 1876 he spoke at Johns Hopkins University:

> I cannot say I am in the slightest degree impressed by your bigness or your material resources as such. Size is not grandeur, territory does not make a nation. The great issue, about which hangs true sublimity, is: What are you going to do with all these things?

Yes, the question is what are we going to do with all these things? Man needs a spiritual interpretation to life in order to use them to the fullest. The farther he progresses the more need does he have for this interpretation of life, because the more technical progress he makes the greater can be the destruction.

A. D. Lindsay in his book, *The Moral Teachings of Jesus,* says,

As an artist can't teach us to paint unless he has first taught us to see, as in all art our power of seeing and hearing and feeling has to grow along with our power of expressing in paint or music or words what we see or hear or feel, so in life.

He is saying that we have to learn to care for the right sort of things. And again:

As it is disastrous when the technique of an artist outruns his power of seeing, so it is in life when our power of realizing our desires outruns our growth in desiring: when we are men in technique and infants in apprehension.

In a real sense we make the kind of world we desire and work for. Marcus Aurelius said, "Every man [and he might have said every civilization] is worth just as much as the things are worth about which he is concerned."

Surely no one can look at our world today with all its madness without the feeling that we are getting the things we do not want, which means that we are desiring the wrong things. If we would have the kind of world we want, we must be willing to change our desires, which will make us over in the process.

Greater than anything else our world needs—greater than skillful diplomacy and technical skill—is to learn to want goodness, to treasure the things of heaven.

And there is only one way to keep our desires and wants high and pure. There is simply not enough goodness in the world to go around; and if there is to be more goodness, it must be obtained from the source of all goodness—God. You cannot maintain noble desires, aspirations, and ideals unless the root that connects them with that which sustains them is left uncut.

Only as men give their allegiance to God, and we believe through Christ, can they be safe in risking their desires and the desires of other men. Getting to know God, trying to understand his will, and attempting to follow it—when such a relationship between men and God predominates in our world, then, and then only, are we safe in the use of our techniques and skills.

AIDS TO WORSHIP

Hymns: "Truehearted, Wholehearted"
          "Take Time to Be Holy"
Scripture: Isa. 2:1-5

A PRAYER

Eternal God, the ground of our being, the source of our strength, the center of our hope, the companion of our way, with gratitude on our lips and praise within our hearts, we laud and magnify thy holy Name. Thou art in nature yet greater than thy nature. Thou art in thy world and yet greater than thy world. Thou art power and yet more than power; mind, and yet more than mind; order, and yet more than order. Thou art love in all its deeper meanings. Our minds are too small to encompass thy nature and our hearts are too feeble to experience thy fullness.

O God:

>   Keep us true;
>   Keep us faithful;
>   Keep us loving;
>   Keep us kind;
>   Keep us brave;
>   Keep us pure;
>   Keep us generous;
>   Keep us humble;
>   Keep us near.

In Jesus' name we pray. AMEN.

27
Finding happiness now
(Thanksgiving)

"THIS IS THE DAY WHICH THE LORD HATH MADE; WE will rejoice and be glad in it."

This little verse of scripture is often used at the opening of morning services. It is a call-to-worship verse that turns our minds Godward. It reminds us that the day is the Lord's. It is his creation, and in it we should be glad and rejoice.

One fine day a man in a church said, "I like that little verse for we should find joy in each day." What philosophy this is, to see in each day that which can make you rejoice, to know that joy should be had now. How we need to make this our very own!

Of course, we as Christians believe that there will be a day "in the sweet by and by" in which our hearts will be made glad. We do believe that for those whose lives have been worthy God will richly reward them with a special welcome at the Gate Beautiful. But today let us think of this verse. Let us look at the possibility of finding happiness now.

Many of us put off finding happiness until some future date. We are tempted to wait for something else to happen, and then we will be happy.

The psychologist William Moulton Marston asked three thousand persons "What have you to live for?" The answers he received revealed that 94 per cent were simply enduring the present, waiting for the future. They were waiting for "something" to happen: waiting for children to grow up, waiting for someone to die. Most of them were waiting for tomorrow, forgetting that all one ever has is today, because yesterday is gone and tomorrow never comes.

The happy person is the person who doesn't put off finding satisfaction in life, but seeks it today. This is expressed in the poem "Happiness" by Priscilla Leonard:

Happiness is like a crystal,
Fair and exquisite and clear,
Broken in a million pieces,
Scattered, scattered far and near.
Now and then along life's pathway,
Lo! some fragments fall;
But there are so many pieces
No one ever finds them all.

You may find a bit of beauty
Or an honest share of wealth,
While another just beside you
Gathers honor, love or health.
Vain to choose or grasp unduly,
Broken is the perfect ball;
And there are so many pieces
No one ever finds them all.

132

Yet the wise as on they journey
Treasure every fragment clear,
Fit them as they may together,
Imagining the perfect sphere.
Learning even to be thankful,
Though their share of it is small;
For it has so many pieces
No one ever finds them all.

Let us look a moment at this line: *Treasure every fragment clear*. It suggests to us to see meaning in every event in life, to try to find joy in life as it moves along.

Too often we are prone to let the distasteful rob us of joy when it can be fitted into the pattern of contented living. Life is made up of its peaks and valleys, its pleasantries and unpleasantries, its joys and its sorrows.

We are not to expect to be forever riding life's crest, to live with a note of merriment every day that comes along. It is the somber note along the way that adds meaning to the bright and brilliant notes of life. It is the hard times that underscore with joy the easy times.

"Treasure every fragment clear." Sometimes with our children we long for them to grow up and get out of our way. A mother imagines what it will be like for baby to grow up. It will mean more freedom. A father dreams of the time when daughter will marry and ease the strain on the meager family income.

As a matter of fact, today is all that we have. We do

133

not know whether we will be given tomorrow. So if we lose the joy of this day, we may not have a chance to experience the joy of tomorrow.

If we could just learn to treasure the fragments of time: the smile of a child, the setting of the sun, the color of a flower garden, the moment of worship.

Someone asked a great man how he accounted for his success, and he answered with a smile, "I had a friend." Friends are free; friendship is available. All of us have at our finger tips the riches in store if we remember this old adage, "Let him who would have friends, first show himself to be friendly." It is a two-way street. Friendship takes time and must be cultivated. Someone once wrote, "Go often to the house of thy friend, for weeds will soon choke the untrodden path.

Friendship is a fragment of life that we should treasure if we are to find happiness.

Then the poet says, *Learning even to be thankful, though their share of it is small*. It is a delusion to believe that only those who have a lot in life are the most thankful or the most happy. Satisfaction in life is not dependent upon substance. Some of the most radiant people we know have little substance; yet they are happy. It makes us think of the little line which goes like this: "If a man is happy, he is not poor."

A person's real wealth consists in the condition of his mind and heart, which makes for happiness. That condition depends upon how thankful he is for what he has.

"Learning even to be thankful, though their share of it is small." What a line, what a way to live! Men who are not grateful will not walk long with God, nor will they have people who will walk long with them. There is no greater virtue than that of gratitude. It is the basis of real satisfaction in life and real happiness.

AIDS TO WORSHIP

Hymns: "Jesus, Thou Joy of Loving Hearts"
"Rejoice, Ye Pure in Heart"
Scripture: Ps. 118:14-24

A Prayer

Most gracious Father, who art never far away from any of us and art found of them that diligently seek thee, we praise thee; we glorify thee; we give thanks unto thee for all thou art to us and all thou dost for us day by day.

Our hearts are filled with thanksgiving:

> For life with all its joys and sorrows, the bitter mingled with the sweet;
> For thy watchful care during hours of darkness;
> For sleep which refreshes the body and mind;
> For light of day and our privilege of working in it;
> For food which fits us for labor and service;
> For friends and loved ones who share life with us;
> For a faith which undergirds and sustains in moments of darkness; and

135

For thy companionship always present to give us
strength.

For all of these things we give thee our hearty thanks.

Speak to our special needs this day. Give to each of us a
sure word, a comforting thought, renewed hope, indefeatable
courage. Without thee, O God, we know not what we would
do. But with thy help and power nothing can shake us,
through Jesus Christ our Lord. AMEN.

28
How to keep Christmas

(*Christmas*)

SOME YEARS AGO A MINISTER SAW A PICTURE OF SANTA Claus blown over by the wind. The gay face of the old man from the north was resting on the floor. As the minister lifted him up gently and set him right again, he had the feeling that Christmas for many people would be blown over after the twenty-fifth. Its gaieties and trimmings would be placed in the closet or attic again, and only the memory would linger in the hearts of millions of people. It would be a memory of trim trees with bright lights, shiny tinsel, and holly with red berries.

For many people this Christmas will be only another holiday. Work will cease for at least twenty-four hours. There will be time for play. There will be no particular reason for celebrating except that everyone else is doing it. What difference will Christmas make for them? Many will return to work, tired and worn. There will be a hollow feeling, an emptiness that comes with spending one's self with no purpose. There will be a cynical wishing that one more day had been allowed for rest.

But there are others who will see in Christmas humanity at its best. They will see the human heart overflow with

137

generosity. The spirit of the season will catch their imagination. They will hurry to and fro buying gifts and sending cards. It will be a joyous time for families to reunite. Baskets will be sent to the poor and trays to the sick. Hearts will be warmed to human need as the best in humanity will be expressing itself.

Yet if Christmas means only this, then it will have been incomplete. To be sure, men will return to their work refreshed by the season and the overflowing good will in human hearts. But there will be no abiding joy.

For Christmas to be real it must be kept as a religious festival, a celebration of the greatest event in history; for indeed it is the supreme date on the world's calendar because it is the anniversary of the world's supreme event. If Christmas is to be abiding joy and strength, we must see in it God expressing himself in human life. We must see in it God making himself known to man in a way man can understand. We must see in Christmas the good news which was brought into the world two thousand years ago, when the true nature of God was revealed in the character of Jesus Christ.

As we approach this season, let us look into the face of the Babe of Bethlehem and see in him God. This to be sure is life's greatest gift—God giving himself to us in a form we can understand.

Seeing in Christmas a religious festival, a celebration of the birth of our Lord, does not mean that we should not have a holiday or see humanity at its best. It does not mean that we should not give gifts, light trees, send cards, unite in families, or share what we have with others.

But all of this must not obscure our sense of the Divine coming into human life, nor must it fatigue our bodies so that God cannot speak to our souls. Let us rejoice in the festivities of the season; let us catch something of man at his best as we give to others; but above all, let us hear the songs of angels and the words of God, for then and then only can we truly keep Christmas. "Fear not: for, behold, I bring you good tidings of great joy, which shall be to all people. For unto you is born this day in the city of David a Saviour, which is Christ the Lord."

AIDS TO WORSHIP

Hymns: "Joy to the World!"
          "There's a Song in the Air!"
Scripture: John 1:1-14

A PRAYER

Eternal God, who in days of old didst make thyself known to prophets and poets, and in the fullness of time didst reveal thyself in thy Son Jesus Christ; help us so to meditate upon thy revelation, that thy constant love may become known to us, and we may feel thy presence always with us.

In the darkness of these days may the light which first appeared over Bethlehem illumine our night. Midst all the rush and strain of the season, grant that we may pause to know that this is a holy season. When the glare and glitter of

139

a secular age would rob us of its deeper meanings, may we remind ourselves whose birthday it is.

Forbid that Christmas should be a time of dread, but rather a season of great joy and a time when Jesus will become a welcome guest in our hearts. In his name we pray. **AMEN.**

INDEX

141

142

143